CONTENTS

CAIN'S REDEMPTION

CAIN'S REDEMPTION

A STORY OF HOPE AND TRANSFORMATION
IN AMERICA'S BLOODIEST PRISON

DENNIS SHERE

NORTHFIELD PUBLISHING
CHICAGO

© 2005 by
NORTHFIELD PUBLISHING

Library of Congress Cataloging-in-Publication Data

Shere, Dennis.
    Cain's redemption : a story of hope and transformation in America's bloodiest prison / Dennis Shere.
      p. cm.
   ISBN-13: 978-1-881273-24-0
    1. Cain, Burl. 2. Louisiana State Penitentiary. 3. Prisons—Louisiana—Angola.
4. Prison wardens—Louisiana—Angola. 5. Criminals—Rehabilitation—Louisiana—Angola. I. Title.

HV9481.A52L687 2005
365'.9763'17--dc22

                                                 2005012811

ISBN: 1-881273-24-5
ISBN-13: 978-1-881273-24-0

1 3 5 7 9 10 8 6 4 2

Printed in the United States of America

*To the men at the Angola Prison
who, forsaking violent pasts, now reach for brighter tomorrows,
sharing faith, becoming their brothers' keepers and committing to
productive pursuits even as they remain incarcerated, often for life.*

*To the staff of the Louisiana State Penitentiary,
hard-working men and women who have embraced
Burl Cain's "moral rehabilitation" strategy to transform
what once was an awful, bloody prison into a place
where inmates can make something of themselves.*

"They are afraid of you. They don't want you in their community. Only with God's help will you change, and without that change you are doomed. You will never leave.
"Now let's change all this . . ."
> —Warden Burl Cain to inmates
> on his arrival at Angola Prison, 1995

Forgetting those things which are behind and reaching forward to those things which are ahead . . .
> —The apostle Paul, in the Bible (Philippians 3:13);
> the verse is carved in stone at Angola's front gate

NOTE FROM THE WARDEN

You might say prisons are in my blood.

My dad, born in 1902, was too old for active duty in World War II. But he wanted to serve, so he worked for the army at Camp Polk (now Fort Polk), near Leesville, Louisiana. German prisoners of war were housed there. My dad had a unique job: he worked in one of the warehouses, and one of his responsibilities was to ensure that the prisoners were provided food and clothing.

The German prisoners were charged with building a concrete highway from Gardner to Alexandria, Louisiana. After the war was over, and as they prepared for the journey back to Germany, they presented my dad with a concrete doll. They had made the doll with concrete, used to build the highway, in appreciation for the way he treated them—stern but fair. When I became a warden in 1981, I remembered Dad's stories about the German prisoners and how he was concerned for our POWs in Germany. He said his job, just as mine is today, was to do the right thing and to do what was expected.

My family's involvement in prison work began with my father during World War II. Dad's philosophy of doing what you can, and doing it well wherever God puts you, is a legacy that I hope I have kept throughout my years as a prison warden. The German doll is my reminder.

—BURL CAIN

PREFACE

Am I my brother's keeper?
– Cain, the firstborn son of Adam

I wasn't sure I was up to writing this book. My background is as a journalist, not a book author. In recent years I also have become an attorney and now work as an assistant public defender. I have brushed up against criminal defendants, a few accused of having killed or maimed. But taking on the assignment of a book about the Louisiana State Penitentiary —more familiarly known as Angola, and once notorious as one of the most brutal, hopeless prisons in America—became for me an opportunity to learn how men survive in prison after conviction.

What I have seen convinces me that society is wrong when it throws away the key. Penitentiaries in this country are little more than warehouses; the human beings inside their walls often lose whatever remaining fragile humanity that they still had before they committed awful crimes.

Yet I wondered whether I could tell a compelling story and keep this account from becoming an uninspiring nuts-and-bolts book about a progressive prison. Journalists, under deadline pressure, tend to strip away most of the colorful details, the word pictures and intensity of the characters about whom they are writing. They concentrate mostly on bare-bone facts, reported in rapid-fire fashion, overlooking intriguing sidelights in the process. I committed to do otherwise, to rise above a staccato recitation, a "just the facts, ma'am" approach. This had to be a highly readable account about a truly incredible prison operated by a one-of-a-kind warden.

But when you hear stories like that, stories of hope and transformation and amazing turnarounds in terrible places, one's natural tendency is skepticism. Who is this Burl Cain, the warden who has gotten so much media attention, not all of it favorable, with his morality-based approach to running a huge Southern prison?

I first met the warden at a breakfast in Chicago. I had agreed to write the book, but only if I believed I could do justice to the story. This was to be an opportunity to assess the warden's vision for the project. I looked forward to gauging the depth of his commitment to making Angola into a peaceful, progressive maximum-security prison, and to determining how he lived out his faith even as he controlled the lives of more than five thousand inmates, most of them serving life sentences without parole.

I also wanted to know if we could achieve a level of trust in each other. I understood that the warden had been burned by a previous book about Angola. I wondered if Cain would be tempted to micromanage this project, if for no other reason than to protect himself and his staff from what he might well believe could become another inaccurate portrayal. Would he allow ready access to inmates, crucial to this story, and permit them to candidly discuss their impressions of life at Angola? Would he insist that I never be left alone as I roamed the prison in search of material for the book? Would he want to read and edit every word I wrote even before the manuscript was finished?

I did not get all of those answers in our initial breakfast meeting. But two incidents, in particular, assured me that any apprehension about the project likely was unfounded. The publishers had presented the warden with a proposed contract, and he had it with him that morning. In bold strokes with a pen, he drew heavy circles around several contract provisions meant to compensate him for his involvement. "I don't want anyone thinking that I am financially benefiting from this book," he insisted. He asked that the publishers turn whatever income it earned over to two ministries.

Later, as we discussed the kinds of positive publicity that the national news media had been giving Angola, the warden turned briefly to the subject of that unflattering book portrayal. I was surprised when he urged me to read it. Most people who have been criticized, as Cain was on that occasion, have little interest in suggesting that a writer read such an account and, perhaps, draw inspiration from it. The warden never asked what I thought of that book, which portrayed Angola as a dismal place. As I explored the prison and talked candidly with staff members as well as prisoners, I found nothing that lent credence to the assertions. I wondered whether the author had intentionally misrepresented the purpose of his book.

As I traveled with the warden throughout Angola, we entered inmate areas without any security officers to provide protection. On occasion, he disappeared briefly as I talked with prisoners. It seemed a bit unsettling at first, coming into contact that way with men serving life sentences for murders and other brutal crimes. There was this recurring thought: These are the worst of the worst. I mean nothing to them. It would take very little effort for someone to take us hostage or hurt us.

But it took little time to feel at peace in Angola—and safer than I sometimes have felt in "free" society. As I accompanied Burl Cain into the prison camps, we were greeted warmly by groups of inmates. They seemed genuinely pleased the warden would take the time to stop by. Cain, in turn, bantered casually with the men, eager to learn what was on their minds. The warden seemed at home, as though the impregnable barriers that a penitentiary must employ to incarcerate did not mean he had to treat these men as inferior or unworthy of his time.

Cain's readiness to listen to the inmates, to accept and sometimes implement their suggestions or fix legitimate complaints, does not suggest that he cannot act harshly or sternly when the occasion demands it. He has had his share of crises, and he has responded appropriately, without apology. One night, I listened as he explained that he was likely to remove an important inmate privilege because someone had abused it. The men accepted the apparent decision without groans or hisses.

It seemed clear that they recognized someone had left the warden with little choice. Cain, for his part, softened the blow by listening as a few inmates offered substitute alternatives. Then he remained off to one side as a few men approached him to voice other personal concerns. He gave them his full attention, seeming to focus exclusively on them as though nothing else of importance mattered at that moment.

The warden of a huge maximum-security penitentiary remains responsible for keeping the peace. The rest—the good programs, the desire to help rehabilitate the inmates—is icing on the cake. He can succeed so long as the place isn't in an uproar. He can give lip service to—and fail to genuinely endorse or incorporate—programs designed to help the inmates. He even can fashion himself after the typical warden portrayed in the movies—someone who talks a good game, claiming to want to help the prisoners, but acting ruthlessly without compassion.

Burl Cain, on the other hand, has demonstrated not only the courage of his convictions but the consistent willingness to carry them out. He believes that men at Angola can rebuild lives shattered by awful crimes if they embrace a genuine change of heart. Therefore, he wants to let the outside world *in*. He wants society to see that many inmates in his prison are being rehabilitated and, perhaps, even could be released someday. He welcomes public scrutiny of what he and his staff are doing. He is always accessible to reporters chasing stories, many of which are not necessarily likely to have happy endings. He has invited a seminary to teach men to become inmate missionaries. He encourages dozens of other outside groups to work with the inmates. He has expanded Angola's annual rodeo. He has attracted organizations to partner with inmates in fulfilling worthwhile community projects. Angola prisoners, for example, now are restoring broken and discarded wheelchairs for Joni Eareckson Tada's Wheels for the World ministry to distribute in Third World countries.

What I have enjoyed most about getting to know Burl Cain is that he has no false piety. He is no saint; he quickly admits he makes his share of mistakes. Like all of us, he sometimes lets his rough edges and occasional inconsistent moments show. He is wise yet crafty, recognizing that a successful warden has to know how to play the political system to get what he needs to operate. He knows how to "work the crowd," readily accepting help from many different quarters, even those with whom he may not be philosophically in agreement.

Cain can be a "good ol' boy," a down-home Southerner spinning compelling and sometimes amusing stories of how he has dealt with incidents at Angola—some of which we will share in this book. He also can wax eloquent about important issues dealing with prison life. He believes, for instance, that some men at Angola, now old and growing increasingly frail, should be set free. But his reasoning is pragmatic as well as compassionate: Angola is running out of room for men whom he calls "predators," who deserve to be locked up in a maximum-security prison.

Burl Cain also enjoys the limelight of being recognized as the warden of Angola.

Yet even as he sometimes intentionally plays to the crowd, he always returns to a sharp focus on the "nonnegotiables." You quickly know what truly matters to him, and on what he will not compromise. One is his zeal for Jesus Christ and his sense that God installed him as warden at Angola for a purpose. Another is the wisdom of his "mama," a woman who warned him that he couldn't just let those men in prison rot away without trying to help them deal with having to spend their lives incarcerated.

Yet another is Cain's belief that he is only as good as the people around him. He insists that he has purposely surrounded himself with prison administrators smarter than he is. The ones I have met clearly fit that description—extremely bright and genuinely committed to Angola. I suspect, though, that the warden is easily the most resourceful and creative of the group, that his team appreciates his unwavering determination to succeed.

The warden often describes men and women with whom he works or comes into contact as the "real deal." By that he is saying their words and actions are consistent—when they say something, they mean it. And they will carry it out without fail. That may be a perfect way to describe Burl Cain.

He is the ultimate "real deal."

—DENNIS SHERE

CHAPTER 1

SAVING ANTONIO

They entered the narrow corridor, father and son, on this morning in late February 1996, and made their way to the tiny cell on Death Row where Antonio James had lived for fourteen years. Sixteen-year-old Marshall Cain was used to the cell blocks, locks, and multiple doors of a maximum-security prison. He'd grown up in that world, grown up making prison rounds with his dad and riding horses with the cowboy inmates working the cattle at the Louisiana State Penitentiary—familiarly known as Angola.

Now he wanted to visit Antonio.

He didn't have much time. In just a few days, James, sentenced to death for killing a man in a New Orleans robbery, would leave his "home" for a final journey. Guards would transport him to a holding cell in Camp F, some distance from the Death Row complex and on the other side of the broad expanse that is Angola.

Shortly before sundown on March 1, guards would escort James from the holding cell into an area where visitors normally congregated with other prisoners on visiting days at the prison. Then they would take the condemned man through a heavily secured metal door, down a short hallway, and at last into a brightly lit but sterile room where he would be strapped to a gurney and put to death by lethal injection.

The teenager, Marshall Cain, had asked his dad, Burl, the warden of Angola who would preside over James's execution, if he could take a plate of homemade chocolate chip cookies to the condemned inmate, now less than a week from his appointment with death. The father, who had come to deeply appreciate how James made the most of his days on Death Row, readily agreed. "I had no idea what kind of interchange might occur between a sixteen-year-old and a man counting off the last days of his life," Burl Cain said later.

Antonio James seemed delighted to see the two visitors. He quickly got up from the cot that he used both for sleeping and as a chair of sorts in which to sit, study, write, and watch the communal television anchored high on a wall across from his cell. He extended his right hand through the bars, and both the warden and his son shook it. They marveled at the upbeat countenance of someone who, it seemed, had so little to look forward to, locked up as he had been in this tiny cell for so many years and now preparing himself, as best he could, to die.

Marshall Cain's eyes momentarily turned away from the man whom society had sentenced to death for what he had done. The teenager began taking mental snapshots of the scene, snapshots he would never forget, absorbing details of Antonio's meager existence. It was such a tiny cell where James lived, about the size of a cage housing wild animals at the zoo, without windows, pictures, or any signs of warmth. There was barely enough room for a thin cot, a small wooden chest in which the inmate stored his belongings, a weathered stainless steel toilet, and small sink with a faded mirror above it. Marshall stifled a shudder.

Then something else caught the teenager's attention. There, on top of the chest, was a worn and much-underlined Bible, Antonio James's most precious possession. The inmate kept it open so he could immediately turn to one of his favorite passages. James would say that it was the

Bible, and its message to him, that not only prepared him to accept his ultimate fate but also served as an encouragement to other Death Row inmates struggling to keep from losing their sanity and flat out giving up. Burl Cain had told his son how this condemned man had come to use his time over the years teaching other Death Row inmates to read so that they, too, might find a measure of hope in a hopeless situation.

Antonio James had dodged death once before when in March 1995, only hours from having his life ended, his attorneys had successfully negotiated a stay of execution. He had tried to make the most of the subsequent time he had left, tried to leave behind something good. But now his additional time was rapidly running out, falling away like the grains of sand slipping through the narrow hole of an hourglass. There was virtually no likelihood James would avoid dying on schedule this time.

Yet here he was, still reaching out to others and now taking a moment to savor the sweet aroma of the cookies he would soon devour. His smiling face offered no hint that the inmate dreaded, or would struggle against when the hour arrived, what the state of Louisiana planned to do to him as final punishment for a killing he helped to commit as a teenager.

"Here," Marshall Cain said as he inserted the paper plate filled with cookies through the narrow slit between the cell bars. James took the plate, sniffed the cookies approvingly, and sampled one. In a moment he turned his attention to the youth.

"Thanks," the inmate said, "that was kind of you. They're my favorites."

Marshall nodded, somewhat self-consciously, then asked a question that clearly reflected both his disbelief and dismay. "Antonio, I have to ask you something. You are a Christian. You care about others; you teach the other inmates to read and you do Bible studies. Why are you here on Death Row? Now my dad has to execute you—why?"

James did not answer for a moment. Then he began to talk about his abusive upbringing, about a father who liked to hurt and belittle him, about escaping by sleeping under the house with his dog keeping him warm. He talked about running away to New Orleans when he was twelve. He and his friends formed a small gang that would rob tourists at gunpoint in the French Quarter. Most of the time, the victims did not resist. Except one. Antonio shot him, and he died. "That's why I'm here," the condemned man said.

"I have some real good advice to you and I hope and pray you will listen and tell your friends. When you get to be fourteen or fifteen years old, your parents will let you start going places with your friends. They will trust you to do the right thing, but it's a jungle out there for young people. There are all kinds of trails, paths, and crossroads. There are lots of bad things that can hurt you in the jungle—bears, tigers, lions. Drugs and alcohol will hurt or destroy you.

"As you go through the jungle with your peers, they will tell you to go here and turn there, but at every crossroad in the jungle, Marshall, if you will just pause, stop, and look for your mom or dad's face—or Jesus' face—it will be there to guide you on the safe path." Antonio told Marshall that all his friends ran away. They testified against him to save themselves and they never visited him. He told Marshall, "Nobody loves you like your mama, daddy, or God. They will always be with you no matter what. They will always keep you safe if you listen and seek their guidance."

ABC television's *Prime Time Live* crew was on-site at Angola producing a documentary on James's execution, entitled "Judgment at Midnight" —so-called because when Cain announces the time of death of an executed man to the media, he makes the statement, "We sent (name's) soul to God for final judgment at (time of death)." ABC's Cynthia McFadden interviewed Marshall after James's execution, saying, "He seemed to be remorseful, a changed man." Marshall responded, "Ms. McFadden, those are the consequences of Antonio's behavior. It's bad, but he can't take back what he did."

James's lawyers had made one final attempt to save his life. Two days before his scheduled execution, the three-person Louisiana pardon board convened at Angola to hear an appeal from the condemned man's attorneys seeking clemency for their client. James was in the room and testified before the board, which listened politely as he apologized for his role in the death of the robbery victim.

"I didn't mean to kill that man," James insisted, as he had throughout his years on Death Row. "But it happened, and I take responsibility for that."

The day before the hearing, James met with the son of the slain man and offered a heartfelt apology for what had happened. The condemned man asked for forgiveness, all the while admitting he could understand if the slain man's son would not grant it. Unsaid, yet implicit, was the hope that the son, now middle-aged, would not only forgive the inmate but would agree that his life should be spared. He accepted James's explanation and apology and declared he had forgiven the inmate. But it seemed clear he would not endorse any effort to stop the execution.

"I'm glad he feels the way he does now, that he's remorseful," the son told a television crew who filmed the meeting. "But he's still got to pay the price."

After a brief closed-door meeting, the pardon board weighing Antonio James's fate emerged into open session and made its findings known to the condemned man, his attorneys, and reporters present to cover the unusual event.

"We find no reason to recommend clemency," the board's chair announced abruptly without further explanation. James stared straight ahead without flinching. His lawyers vowed to continue fighting to stop his execution. Their faces betrayed a bitter disappointment; only hours later, when it became apparent that nothing could save their client, did the attorneys break down and weep.

The pardon board's decision all but guaranteed the execution would proceed on schedule. Only the Louisiana governor's direct intervention, a stay issued by the state's highest court, or some action by the U.S. Supreme Court would stop the execution now. It seemed unlikely that any miracle might yet occur to keep Antonio James from dying.

As the date of his death drew near, Antonio asked the warden lots of questions. "How is it when you die? What happens to your soul, and how does it really work?" Cain listened, taking the man's questions seriously. He quoted Jesus' words to the thief hanging next to Him on the cross: "Today you will be with me in paradise."

He also told Antonio what Billy Graham, in his book *Angels,* says about those celestial beings and how they escort the redeemed soul to heaven. Antonio asked Cain if he would hold his hand when the time came, so he would be connected to this earth while he reached into heaven with the other hand. Cain promised he would.

On the afternoon of March 1, 1996, the condemned man and his family gathered in the visitors' room in the death house for their final farewell. They sat around a long table, laughing and reminiscing. Eventually the warden walked in, and the family's attention shifted to him.

He spoke briefly. "Thank you for coming so Antonio can say good-bye. I know how much he appreciates it." He did not add, nor did it need to be said, that he applauded Antonio's mother, siblings, nieces, and nephews for being brave enough to offer unconditional love to him at the time he needed it most.

As he left, Cain stared at James, who acknowledged his glance. "I'll be seeing you shortly," the warden said quietly. It was time for Antonio to prepare for his last meal.

Burl Cain had done his best to prepare Antonio James for death. The two men had spoken often about the events soon to unfold, most recently just that day. The warden had explained what would happen when he would arrive to escort the inmate from his holding cell to the death chamber. He spared no detail, believing James would be helped by knowing exactly how things would play out.

The warden described the concrete block death chamber and the gurney, positioned diagonally inside the room. He told James how a guard team, specially trained and rehearsed, would buckle him securely to the gurney and how an EMT would insert a needle into each of his arms. Cain explained that only one needle would be needed to administer the lethal combination of drugs, but the second one would be in place in case the first failed. Cain made it clear that he would try as hard as he could to ease James's departure from this world.

The inmate listened intently, taking everything in without interrupting, almost as though the procedure were meant to help, not put him to death. The calm expression on Antonio's face did not change as Cain explained what was going to happen.

"Any more questions?" the warden asked. Antonio shook his head. "Let's pray together, then," said Cain.

"I'd appreciate that very much," Antonio said.

The warden reached out and grasped the inmate's hand as he whispered: "Dear God, You're about to welcome Antonio into Your kingdom. Help him to keep his focus entirely on You during the coming hours. Help him to realize that he is about to come into the presence of Jesus. And Father, we just pray for the victim's family, that You'll be with them and comfort them . . ."

The ABC television crew filmed Antonio's last walk. He needed no assistance as he was led from the holding cell and through the area where he had had dinner with Cain, Assistant Warden Darrel Vannoy, his spiritual advisor, and several others. When James entered the death chamber he paused at the microphone and addressed the witnesses. He told the victim's family he was sorry and asked their forgiveness. He turned, looked at the execution gurney, walked over to it, sat on the side and lay down.

The efficient strap-down team did their work in ninety seconds, securing leather straps around the prisoner's ankles, thighs, abdomen, chest, and shoulders. Then the executioner began searching for a vein in his right arm into which he could insert the needle.

"Antonio was so calm, his pulse so low, that we couldn't locate a suitable vein even when he made a fist," Cain said later. "He apologized for making things difficult. The EMT slapped his arm to see if he could raise a vein. That didn't work, so finally we inserted the needle into his leg."

Now, with every step of the procedure accomplished, the warden signaled for the curtain to open so the witnesses could observe the actual execution. Cain took hold of Antonio's hand and stared into his eyes. Then he said, "Antonio, the chariot is here; get ready for the ride. Here we go; you are about to see Jesus."

In a gesture that the warden took to mean that he fully understood and expected to see his Lord, James squeezed Cain's hand. Then the warden turned toward a one-way glass. He could not see the executioner who would administer the drugs, but he could give the signal.

Cain nodded.

The process, irrevocable, began. In a moment, the first drug began to enter Antonio James. The inmate breathed two deep breaths, relaxed his grip on Burl Cain's hand, and closed his eyes for the last time. The lawyers had tears in their eyes.

Later that night, in front of TV cameras, the warden would announce that "we have sent Antonio James to his final judgment." He purposely avoided using the words "execution" and "death."

The warden's compassion in directing executions does not mean that he opposes capital punishment. He makes no public statements about the death penalty. As warden, he is committed to carrying out the sentences that Louisiana juries and judges hand out, whether to send inmates to Angola for a period of years, for life without parole, or to their deaths.

Some victims' family members—but not all—have criticized Cain for the way he conducts executions. They say he should dispense justice without becoming involved in the slightest in the lives of the men he is putting to death.

"They say that I seem more interested in their loved one's killer than I do in the victim," the warden remarked. "I say that you have to do *what* you can *where* you are. I wish I could have been there to hold the *victim's* hand: just because I couldn't be there when your daughter died, for example, doesn't mean I shouldn't be there when her killer is put to death."

Cain, in fact, often expresses great sympathy for the victim's families. "I regret there *had* to be a victim," he says.

James was the second of six men whom the warden has executed. James's death showed him how important it is to give every inmate, even those condemned to die and waiting for years on Death Row before their executions, an opportunity to find meaning to their existence in prison even in the direst circumstances. For the warden, that existence is found in believing in Jesus Christ as Savior. Not every inmate who has died in the execution chamber during Cain's tenure at Angola has made that commitment. One inmate, a Buddhist, whispered to Cain as the execution began, "Tell my lawyer he's fired."

The executions he has conducted have served, along with other events, to motivate Cain to continue making sweeping changes to a prison culture at Angola that for years had been among the most violent in the nation. It would encourage him to take risks—although he refuses to call them that. He would offer inmates, most of them serving sentences from which they will never be set free, the chance to join a "community" where they could begin to experience what Cain would come to call "moral rehabilitation."

CHAPTER 2

"YOU JUST KILLED THAT MAN"

Antonio's execution was different from the first one Burl Cain presided over.

He had been on the job at Angola for only three months when the prison received a death warrant on one Thomas Ward, imprisoned for murdering his mother-in-law. Cain had witnessed an execution by electrocution but had no experience with lethal injection. Still, his staff was experienced. He wasn't worried. He planned merely to do his part in the procedure. He did not plan to speak to the condemned man ahead of time, save a perfunctory meeting to describe what would happen the night of his death. Cain saw Ward as little more than a criminal whom society had ruled should die for his crime. "I was brash, bold, and cocky," he says now. "I thought I knew it all. I didn't go to his last meal. I didn't worry about what he must have been experiencing in the hours before his death. I just thought about what I had to do to execute him. We'd do it right, by the book. The procedure would be a success in my mind if there were no hitches."

The execution was set for midnight. Cain and several security officers trained to carry out the execution entered the condemned man's cell a few minutes before the appointed time. Thomas Ward had gone to pieces emotionally.

"He couldn't walk, so we carried him in an upright position from the holding cell to the death chamber. There was fear on his face. You could see so clearly just how frightened he was. He didn't utter a word as we strapped him to the gurney. When the time came to ask him if he had anything to say, he didn't answer. He choked up."

The warden stood beside the gurney and peered through the little one-way window at the executioner behind the window, who would release first a sedative to knock out the inmate, then two drugs that would stop his heart and cause him to die. Cain checked his watch to see if midnight had arrived.

Angola used to use an electric chair for executions, but it was abandoned when critics of capital punishment convinced the Louisiana legislature that death by lethal injection was more humane. Aside from the gurney on which the defendant is secured, and two red telephones on the wall for the warden to accept any last-minute reprieve from the governor or the DOC, the room is well lit and sterile, without furniture or any decorative distractions.

Later, after Antonio James died, an inmate asked and received permission to paint murals on two walls in a reception area on the way to the execution chamber—murals of Elijah on a fiery chariot rising to heaven and Daniel, without fear, in the lions' den.

The time had come.

"We had settled on a code word—Exodus—and I gave a thumbs-down gesture. (If one of the red phones rang, the first word had to be 'Exodus' or I would hang up the phone.)

"The inmate's face was a mask of fear. I could see the chemicals rushing through the narrow tube and into his arm. He breathed two breaths— *pssh, pssh*—and closed his eyes. In five minutes he was gone."

The thought came over Cain: You just killed that man. You said nothing to him about his soul. What does God think of you?

Later that night, after Cain met with news reporters to announce the execution, a local funeral home picked up the prisoner's body, and the necessary paperwork surrounding the execution had been completed, the warden got into his car and drove through the front gate leading out of Angola.

"When I left the prison, the scene I just had witnessed was still in my mind. I couldn't sleep. I had just seen someone killed. I had picked the time of his death. I had given a thumbs-down, and he had died."

As he drove toward his home shortly after 1:00 a.m., the warden began to realize the full impact of what he had done. He deeply regretted that he had sent someone to death without ever giving him a chance to make peace with God.

"My mama's words, when I became the warden at Angola, kept ringing inside my head. She had told me, 'You're responsible to see that they have the opportunity to know Jesus—and you didn't do anything you should have done to prepare that prisoner for his death.'"

Cain had a hard time sleeping that night. He desperately needed to talk to his pastor about his sorrow over his part in the execution. How, he wondered, does a man of faith carry out an execution?

Walking under live oak trees outside the church, pastor Woody Markett first quoted a passage from Genesis: "He who sheds man's blood so shall his blood be shed." That didn't satisfy Cain. "Look," he said, "you have to give me something from the *New* Testament—they killed all kinds of people in the Old Testament."

"Reverend Woody," as Cain called him, then quoted Paul's letter to the Romans (13:1–6) where he described the role of rulers. He equated Cain's job as warden to that of a ruler devoting himself to bringing judgment on those who commit evil. But he also asked Cain if he had thought to tell the condemned man about Jesus, to give him something that might save his soul in his last hours on earth.

"I had to admit, shamefully, that I hadn't done that," Cain said later.

Burl Cain decided right then that never again would he put someone to death without telling that man about his soul and about Jesus. He would not insist that the man had to listen to him, and he would stop if the man rejected his message. But, at the very least, he would open the door.

The warden also made another strategic decision. No longer would he set the time for a man's death. The execution would occur in God's time, in a window between 6:00 and 9:00 p.m., based on the moment when the sun set. Cain had been deeply troubled when he happened to be at the governor's mansion the day of Ward's execution and learned that some of the state troopers on security detail bet on the exact time of the execution. The "winner" was the officer who most closely guessed the actual time that the condemned man was put to death.

"A trooper came up to me before the execution and asked what time I planned to put the inmate to death," Cain said, noting that Louisiana law gave him a three-hour window of time on execution day in which to carry out the death sentence.

"I asked him why he wanted to know and the guard said, 'We're betting on the exact time. Do you think you might do it at ten minutes after midnight?' Right then, I made a decision. I would no longer carry out a death sentence on my time. I would carry it out according to God's time, in the dark when the sun set. Then the inmate would know that I was not going to come to get him on my time, on a whim." The Louisiana legislature passed a law changing the time of executions.

One other execution changed the way Cain ran his prison.

The man sentenced to die, Feltus Taylor, had previously been incarcerated at another prison and released after serving his sentence. He had gotten a job at a local fast-food fried-chicken outlet but had been fired; however, the manager had told him he would help the ex-offender find another job.

He returned a couple of days later under the pretext of looking at jobs in the paper with manager Keith Clark. In reality, Taylor needed money and planned to rob the store. He waited around until the last customer had left, then pulled out a small pistol and forced manager Clark and a young female server named Donna Ponsano into the cooler and ordered them to kneel. Then he shot them both in the head. Donna died on the spot, but Clark survived—paralyzed from the neck down.

When police checked the records of the store's employees and former workers, they zeroed in on and arrested Feltus Taylor. At his trial he was found guilty of first-degree murder, and the jury recommended death. He arrived at Angola, where he spent years on Death Row as his attorneys fought to keep him from being executed. During that time Taylor, said Cain, became a Christian. When his appeals ran out, the state set an execution date and it came most suddenly.

Taylor's family came to visit on the day of the execution. As 3:00 p.m. approached, they became very emotional, as that was the time they would have to leave the visiting area in the death house. (At Angola, families of both the condemned man and the victim are provided with a private waiting area with TV and refreshments—something new under Cain's leadership.) Cain asked the family to be strong as they departed, because Feltus needed to be as emotionally and spiritually ready as he could be as his final hours drew near.

"I met with Feltus, and we prayed together. When the time came, we took him into the death chamber and prepared him for the execution. I asked him if he had anything he wanted to say. He couldn't hardly talk, and he didn't say he was sorry for what he had done."

One of the witnesses observing the scene through a window to the execution chamber was Keith Clark. Confined to a wheelchair, Keith had met with the warden in the hours before Taylor's death. They talked about the inmate's decision to commit his life to Jesus Christ. And Keith Clark said something that amazed Burl Cain.

Now, standing next to Taylor as he lay on the execution gurney, the warden bent over and shared a last-minute conversation in a whisper with the inmate. "I held his hand and told him to get ready to see Jesus' face. He looked up into my eyes and said, 'Will you tell Keith Clark that I'm sorry for what I did to him and Donna?'

"I nodded yes. Then I told him, just as his eyes began to close for the last time, 'Keith told me that he forgives you.'" Feltus smiled, closed his eyes, breathed two breaths, and then the breathing stopped.

The road was dark and quiet as Cain drove home later, troubled by the suffering he had seen that day. A young woman was in the grave, a man in a wheelchair, families destroyed—all, he reflected, because a selfish, sinful man wanted to steal a few dollars. The correctional system had failed. The criminal justice system had failed—with tragic results.

There had to be a better way.

That night Burl Cain vowed to himself that he would do all in his power to transform the men under his charge. It would be worth all the effort, he thought, if even one person was saved from being a victim of violent crime.

In Cain's words:

"As my career as a warden evolved, I had come to realize that criminals are very selfish people. It is so simple to understand. They take your life, your property, anything they want for themselves. They don't ask. They just sneak around, lie, steal, kill, whatever they want.

"I realized that I could teach them to read and write, could help them learn skills and a trade—but without moral rehabilitation, I would only be creating a smarter criminal."

And so Burl Cain's vision for transforming Angola began to unfold—in a place where anything resembling hope and morality had been in desperately short supply for a very long time.

Chapter 3

LIFE ON THE MISSISSIPPI

Angola can feel oddly serene and pastoral.

At night, standing on top of a rising hillside near the main gate, a visitor can believe he's seeing the yellow-orange lights of a handful of tiny villages dotting the pitch-black darkness of the farmland surrounding them. It is something like the view an airline passenger has peering out the window of a commercial jet as it makes a nighttime landing approach. Little towns come into view, twinkling in the blackened landscape.

So it is at Angola. The night air is cool and nearly soundless. Occasionally, in the distance the headlamps of a vehicle traveling the terrain glimmer in the darkness, barely illuminating the narrow road stretching out ahead. Standing there, overlooking the prison grounds, one is overcome by a strange sense of peace. It is hard at the moment to imagine those little brightly lit "villages"—isolated prison camps surrounded by high fences, barbed wire, and guard towers—house thousands of men who have killed or committed other atrocities. The worst of the worst. Ninety percent of the prisoners will die here, because the state of Louisiana's draconian sentencing laws almost never allow for parole. The average sentence is eighty-eight years; the prison population comprises men convicted of first- or second-degree murder, aggravated sex crimes, armed robbery, or habitual felony.

And they are well, well away from civilization. When the sun comes up over the pastoral expanse, you see a facility on the banks of the Mississippi that spreads over eighteen thousand acres of lush agricultural acreage where cotton and food crops grow easily—corn, soybeans, vegetables. Two thousand head of cattle graze the grounds. The vast land is worked by teams of inmates under the watchful eye of a mounted and armed guard. The first people to benefit from the bounty of the land were the Tunica Indians, who ranged in the area for centuries. The great river would flood the flatlands, driving game into the rugged hills with their deep ravines and thick undergrowth. When the water receded, fish would be left trapped in potholes and ditches, making them easily accessible to Indians.

They say that this maximum-security prison is about the same size, in landmass, as the isle of Manhattan. Like Manhattan, Angola is surrounded by water on three sides, sitting on about fourteen miles of river frontage. The Mississippi's rapid current serves as an awesome buffer—and a warning to inmates considering escape.

The majestic river rises every spring and sometimes overflows its banks and the massive earth levees protecting prison property. In 1997, much of Angola was underwater, forcing Burl Cain and his staff to relocate many inmates—the ones in dormitories—to a "tent city" on high ground. The more dangerous prisoners, locked away in one-story jail cells, fretted the waters might engulf them and they would drown. Cain knew he would not open the jail cells but did not say so aloud—to do so would have sparked a riot among fearful prisoners.

Instead, he devoted all of his energy to directing a combined effort by the inmates and staff to shoring up vulnerable levees with sandbags. During an all-night vigil, the warden drove a surplus army troop carrier loaded with sandbags and urged everyone not to give up. They kept the great river at bay—just. The U.S. Army Corps of Engineers authorized increasing the height of the levees by six feet, enough to withstand the river even if it rose to historic flood levels.

The fourth side of Angola, the one facing toward the nearest town, St. Francisville, some twenty miles away, is largely unpopulated forestland, carpeted with dense underbrush and mined with poisonous snakes. It, too, serves as a buffer against escape.

You can drive the roads inside Angola and, if you ignore the presence of the widely spaced prison camps, believe for the moment that you are out in the country passing through serene farmland and past an inviting, well-stocked fishing lake. There are cattle and horses, and there are men working the fields, driving farm machinery, repairing equipment, maintaining bushes and flowers and trees in full bloom. From a distance, the workers look to be farmers, not prison inmates.

Only when a farm crew comes into sight is it apparent that these men are not here by choice—nor do they work in the fields by choice. The only correctional officers inside the prison who are armed are the ones astride horses in the farm fields. They carry rifles. Even more important, they carry two-way radios to call for help when there is danger, when a fight develops between inmates, or someone makes an ill-advised run for freedom.

An inmate attempting to escape from a farm detail is foolish. They have nowhere to flee and hide. The prison's chase team, with dogs, horses, and even military vehicles at its disposal, is trained to relentlessly pursue an escapee and will not give up until the man is cornered.

The prison camps, those brightly lit small villages dotting the night, can be seen more clearly in the light of day. They are not as ominous-looking as you might imagine from movies like *The Shawshank Redemption* or old prison films you might see on TV. Buildings are mostly single-story cinder-block structures painted cream and off-white. Each camp has recreational areas and a few picnic benches to sit on when the prisoners are outside on work breaks.

Yet these prison camps—seven in all, Main Prison C, D, F, and J, RC/Death Row, and Dog Pen—are anything but benign. If a prison does nothing else well, it must ensure that the prisoners within cannot get out. High fences lined with razor-sharp wire enclose each facility. At strategic intervals along the fences stand guard towers, manned around the clock. The outside spotlights are on throughout the night, affording few shadows in which an inmate can hide or cause trouble outside the watch of the correctional officers inside the towers or on duty within the camp.

Even with all the wide-open space to monitor, the inmates are tightly controlled. No one goes anywhere without permission, and no one ever disappears from the "radar screen." After a visitor passes through the outer gate and into a camp, he still must clear guard stations and enter inmate areas through heavy metal doors. Once inside, he may come upon a dormitory, cell blocks, the visitors' room, or the mess hall, where inmate cooks prepare meals. Every movement from one area to another inside a camp requires the inmate to stand and wait for a correctional officer to grant access. As you wait, the nighttime vision of a peaceful, pastoral village fades in the daytime reality.

Still, the prisoners within the camps appear to have some measure of freedom of movement. They are not handcuffed or in chains. They do not wear striped prison outfits. Most are dressed in white or gray T-shirts and denim blues with gym shoes. They seem more comfortably dressed than the blue-uniformed guards who carefully keep track of them. Most of the camps have both single-bunk dormitories and double-man cell living quarters. One camp, J, is for the worst of the worst of the worst, housing prisoners who break the rules and cause trouble. Most of the 480 inmates at J live in single cells. Some are in total isolation. Entrance to their cells requires a visitor to pass through two sets of steel doors. The occupants of these—who insist on acting out their frustration inappropriately, sometimes even trying to throw human waste at the guards (which is not tolerated and brings about stiffer penalties)—cannot communicate with others except by passing notes. "We don't permit shouting," Cain says. "We control the noise level; we don't want a loud prison."

No one winds up in Camp J by accident, and no one stays in Camp J unless he refuses to shape up. The facility is not so much a place of punishment as it is an agent of change. There are single cells, to isolate troublemakers, within each of the camps. But J is where most behavior modification takes place. Occasionally, even a Death Row inmate is held temporarily at J when he won't cooperate. He soon finds that the spartan quarters he "enjoyed" on Death Row are plush compared to what is made available to him at J.

Some inmates spend their entire existence at Angola inside designated camps, except for times each day when they are let out under guard to perform various chores, particularly in the farm fields. Many eventually become trustees, a status that allows them to work with minimal guard supervision anywhere on the prison grounds. Some even venture, with supervision, outside Angola. Inmate gospel bands perform at fairs, festivals, and nursing homes throughout Louisiana. Inmate trainers teach "free people" to perform CPR rescues. Inmate preachers occasionally are invited to speak at area churches.

The trustees are men whose exemplary conduct has earned them the right to make up to twenty cents an hour, rather than the four cents paid to ordinary inmates. There are three classifications of trustees: A, the highest, B, and C. Trustees are expected to set an example for other inmates to follow. They must toe the line and avoid being disciplined, or written up, for various infractions.

It takes an inmate about ten years to become a trustee. If he follows the rules, he can maintain that role for the rest of his time at Angola. A major slipup can send him skidding back down virtually to beginning inmate status, and, perhaps, even a stint in isolation at Camp J. Then he must start over with the process of becoming a trustee. That can take years —but these men have plenty of time.

Most, sentenced to life, may wind up in prison for fifty or more years before they die or, by the equivalent of a miracle, win a pardon. Even those with determinate sentences will spend at least forty years at the prison;

otherwise, they do not come to Angola but serve their time at one of Louisiana's other prisons.

Many of the inmates will die here. The lifespan of a prisoner is shorter than it would be if he were on the outside. Prison life, no matter how Angola's administrators work to create a peaceful community atmosphere, is hard. Real freedom is impossible within a prison, no matter how progressive its staff is or how compliant the inmates are. Living in tight quarters, even in the more loosely run dormitories, causes tensions that sometimes fester between prisoners. It takes inmates a long time to fully trust each other—if ever. Too many predators are eager to take advantage of a weak prisoner. Relationships begin and thrive only when inmates become committed to their mutual faith or become involved in like-minded activities. Until then, the only bond is a negative one—each man knows that the inmates around him have committed awful crimes, as he has. They may share "jailhouse lawyer" talk, aimed at figuring out ways to appeal their sentences, but little else at first.

Even though the food is nourishing and health care has improved dramatically at Angola, inmates grow old before their time, transformed from youth to middle age to inevitable sparse white hair and deeply lined faces. They become sick and must be cared for. They die, often young and sometimes suddenly, from heart attacks or strokes, or over time, from cancer or other debilitating diseases.

Angola has access to free-people hospitals in Baton Rouge and New Orleans. An inmate whose kidneys are shutting down can be transported to the Dixon Correctional Institution three times a week for dialysis. But he can't get a transplant, regardless of sentence, due to the cost. Some diseases, curable on the outside, are held at bay for a time before overwhelming an inmate ineligible for the care available to a free person.

To the outside world, Angola's residents will always be dismissed as killers who do not deserve to be freed again. The challenge for many men at the prison becomes demonstrating that something about their lives is worth noting and applauding. That's in large part why many of them become proficient at making crafts for the hobby shows connected with

Angola's annual rodeos. They want the public to see them as having worth and value despite what they have done that got them sent to the prison in the first place. It also is why they gravitate to programs operated within the prison. As the inmates show they are interested in what these groups have to offer, they send a subtle but unmistakable message: We're not ogres or monsters. We may have done terrible things, but we are changing, and you are helping us.

For others, prison life is merely to be endured. They often remain "predators," as Burl Cain describes them, and they may not adapt to prison life easily, nor do they give in without a fight. They do only what they have to do to get by and they are always tempted to disobey the rules, even when they know they probably won't get away with it.

The prison staff works hard to identify and control the predators, all the while giving increasing opportunity to the inmates who genuinely try to fit in. And the opportunities to fit in are many—from working in a bike shop, to serving as an inmate counselor or paralegal, to learning how to fix machinery, to helping as a hospice volunteer. None, of course, are gateways to the vast freedom that the outside world enjoys. But at the very least, they provide to those who take advantage of them a meaningful life within what once was an oppressive and frightening prison environment.

This fear and oppression was what Burl Cain set out to change when he arrived at Angola in 1995. Cain has observed that the vast, lush land on a bend of the lower Mississippi has seen more human suffering than any other place in America, beginning with its roots as a slave-breeding plantation— where the "crop" was human beings, found to be more profitable than raising cotton or indigo or sugar cane. Angola was so named because the owner believed the "best" slaves came from that African country. After the Civil War, the plantation owner contracted with the state of Louisiana to house state prisoners for free. Prisoners worked the farm and helped build the Mississippi levee system to New Orleans, using mules and wheel-barrows. When a prisoner died, he was buried right in the levee and work continued—meaning the overseers had less dirt to haul. About 10 percent of the prisoners died every year from disease or malnutrition.

Even after the state assumed control of the prison in 1901, the law of the jungle prevailed on the river. Inmates formed gangs for protection, with members sleeping in shifts as protection from predators. Some inmates put magazines under their shirts for armorlike protection in the event someone tried to stab them while they slept. Shorthanded prison staffs were for all intents and purposes forced to stand helplessly by and watch events spiral out of control. For a while, some inmates even served as guards, carrying rifles and administering uneven and preferential discipline. Inmates were shoehorned into cells or multilevel cots wedged into small rooms. The food and medical treatment provided was marginal, enough to keep an ailing prisoner alive—barely. Many died before their time.

In the 1970s, angry inmates, realizing that they were enduring a terrible injustice, filed habeas corpus complaints seeking to change the prison's atmosphere. The basis for their objections was that serving time in prison was their punishment, not having to struggle to survive in inhumane conditions at Angola. A federal judge in Baton Rouge, Louisiana's capital, read the inmates' petitions and decided they were right.

In effect, he took control of the prison.

The judge required the state of Louisiana to invest in upgrading the frightful physical facilities. He ordered the state to hire enough staff members to disarm inmate guards and install a civilian administration that could protect prisoners, many of whom never went to sleep without a weapon beneath their pillows to fend off vicious assaults, launched without warning, by other inmates. At the time the judge took over, Angola was regarded as one of the nation's notorious prisons, on a par with California's San Quentin, Parchman Penitentiary in Mississippi, and New York's fabled Sing Sing.

Slowly conditions at Angola improved, yet the focus remained on warehousing the fifty one hundred inmates, most of them sentenced to life without parole. That effectively meant that most defendants entering the prison were never going to get out, unless somehow they might escape, or convince an appellate court of their innocence, or most miraculously, obtain a rare recommendation for pardon from a state board.

The handful of prisoners serving life, whose conduct at Angola merited serious consideration of a pardon, rarely received one. In short, a man sentenced to the Louisiana State Penitentiary for life could expect to live there until he died. Somehow, then, he had to learn to accept a strictly regimented life under conditions that, while improved, offered little in the way of rehabilitation or training. In a very real sense, his punishment within the grounds of Angola became magnified and extended because of the bleak, largely hopeless existence he faced.

In 1995, a new warden came to Angola, into a job he had no desire to accept but one that he could not turn down. Someone said, "There are demons over this place." Cain said, "I'm going to run them off, with God's help." (Chris Frink, "Breaking into Prison," ChristianityToday.com)

Burl Cain became a warden by accident. He had gone to Louisiana State University to major in vocational agricultural education. When he graduated, he took a job with the state helping to oversee farming operations at various Louisiana prisons. That led, improbably, to an offer in 1981 to serve as warden of the Dixon Correctional Institution, a medium-security facility with about fourteen hundred inmates located about thirty miles from Angola. When he called his mother to tell her the news, she said, "That's good. You just remember one thing. I raised you right—to know God—and God will hold you accountable one day. If you don't see that those prisoners have a chance to know Him, He will hold you accountable for their souls."

On Cain's first day at Dixon, he scheduled a meeting with the staff, as is customary for a new warden. However, he told his new secretary to put the chaplains in a separate room. When he arrived at the prison, instead of going to the meeting room where the deputy warden and all the ranking officers were waiting, Cain went to the room where the chaplains had gathered. It was a short meeting and to the point. He told them he would divide the prison population into equal parts, giving each their share: this would be their flock of sheep. He told them what his mother had told him. "You are the shepherds of your flocks," he said. "If the flocks don't grow, I'll get other shepherds."

That was it. Despite resistance from correctional officers called "the demon at the gate" that wouldn't let inmates out for worship services or let volunteers in to do prison ministry, Cain's early efforts at moral rehabilitation began to bear some fruit.

Prisons, of course, aren't administered in a vacuum. Cain was still at Dixon in 1991 when the wardens of all the Louisiana prisons formed an organization called LAWS (Louisiana Wardens and Superintendents). Previous governors had appointed a banker and a farm-seed salesman to manage the state corrections program. "These appointments were disastrous—good men who knew nothing at all about corrections or rehabilitation," Cain comments. "We wardens wanted our boss to be a professional, one of us, and we chose as our candidate Richard Stalder, a brilliant young warden at Wade Correctional Center in Homer, Louisiana"—at the time the only prison in Louisiana accredited by the American Correctional Association.

Stalder had achieved this, Cain says, with "no help" from state corrections headquarters, and he had been Cain's deputy warden at Dixon Correctional Institute. Cain, president of LAWS, and the other prison officials decided Stalder was their man. Cain scheduled a meeting with Stalder and gubernatorial candidate (and former governor) Edwin Edwards at Ruth's Chris Steakhouse in Baton Rouge. Stalder, who loved being a warden, said it was a bad time for him and he didn't want to come. Cain rescheduled the meeting and told Stalder, "You can't cancel meetings with a former governor; and anyway, he might win, and then what . . ."

The former governor's assistant made the ground rules clear: the time they were to meet, the table they were to sit at, and that Cain and Stalder were to pay. "It was a fun meeting," Cain recalls. "The governor asked all kinds of crazy questions about prison and prison life. He wanted to know about escapes, bloodhounds, and how we manage homosexuals. The other

amusing thing was, he would eat out of our plates. He ate some of my vegetables and part of Richard's dessert." The colorful Edwards liked to tell
jokes, but all the while he was also sizing Stalder up. At the end of dinner
that night he told Stalder that if elected, he would appoint him as secretary
of corrections – but that many times he would not believe he would get the
job. Which is exactly what happened: "For months during and after the
election," says Cain, "we heard of all these different people who would be
appointed, only for Richard to get the call one day. The governor kept his
word, but worried us to death."

Stalder's appointment was a true turning point in the history of corrections in the state. He appointed as his undersecretary James Le Blanc,
whom Cain terms a "genius" at managing the department's budget. "Both
Stalder and Le Blanc brought integrity and honesty to a new level in
Louisiana corrections," Cain says of his close friends. Le Blanc later suc-
ceeded Burl Cain as warden at Dixon Correctional Institute—a place Cain
says he didn't really want to leave.

"My life at DCI was good," he says. "I had a wonderful staff, many
of whom are now at Angola. DCI was smaller, and if I had a really prob-
lematic inmate I could just send him to Angola."

When the then-warden of Angola, John Whittley, retired in January
1995 and Secretary Stalder named Cain his successor, Cain saw it as a
temporary posting, thinking Stalder himself should be Angola's warden
after his stint in Baton Rouge. Stalder, an old friend, had encouraged Cain
to move from education to corrections years previously, and Cain trusted
his counsel. As it turned out, however, the Louisiana Ethics Board ruled
that Stalder could not appoint himself as Angola warden—so Cain had to
accept the job on a permanent basis.

"That was scary," Cain said later, "because Whittley had told me,
'About five years is as long as you can survive at Angola. Bad things just
happen.'"

When Cain arrived at Angola, the public mentality concerning
prisoners was truly "lock 'em up and throw away the key." People on the
outside were scared of prisoners. They wanted them put away. What

happened after that, after the gates slammed shut, was of no concern to those on the outside.

Burl Cain and the team he surrounded himself with vowed to change all that, to create a new prison, a better prison—a place where men sentenced to life could make lives and homes for themselves.

Cain knew it wouldn't be good enough to maintain a tight lid on a maximum-security prison so that the place didn't blow apart. He realized he had to foster a positive "culture of community" in a place where fighting and fear and apathy and the gospel of "every man for himself" ruled the day.

When he arrived at Angola, he outlined his philosophy to the inmates: Your dormitory is like a city or community. The beds are houses along a "street," the aisle; three beds down is really three doors down. You should visit your neighbors, talk to each other, console each other, be concerned about each other's well-being. Keep your "city" free of drugs, violence, and other illegal activity. Don't steal from your neighbor. Go to church together. Don't use profanity. Once you start cursing each other out, violence is likely to follow.

The typical prison culture is a "turn your head" culture. "Live and let live; if it doesn't affect me, then I don't care." This was the mentality Cain set out to transform. When some inmates would argue that they should not be held accountable for the actions of others, he would point to the neighborhood-watch model. "If you see someone dealing drugs on your street corner, do you turn your head? No, you call the authorities to report it. You don't want your community to become a gang-controlled haven for lawlessness, unsafe for family living. Well, that's the way it is here."

Of course, the warden realizes that many of the communities his inmates are most familiar with are "gang-controlled havens for lawlessness" where criminals are trained for prison life and shuttle from streets to prison to streets to prison—like Feltus Taylor. Positive change, therefore, has to start behind the prison walls, because it won't happen on the streets.

And, in a community of men in for murder and rape and armed robbery, positive change is always threatened.

Any prison fights a constant battle to keep drugs off the premises, and Angola is no exception. Cain says to the skeptics that as important as it is to build a positive, moral culture in a prison, "It's kinda like fishing: you can't catch 'em all but you have to keep fishin'." Recently prison staff caught three inmates smoking marijuana while working at the woodworking hobby shop in Camp F. The shop was immediately closed and locked tight. As Cain walked through the camp, the inmates grumbled, "You shouldn't punish us for what others do wrong."

"Someone should have told us drugs were in the hobby shop," he replied. "You know the policy. Where are the good citizens?"

Cain was disturbed. Angola had come so far. He wanted the men to be able to work, to be able to learn new skills, and create beautiful things to sell at Angola's spring rodeo. "You can see the inmate's face just light up when you tell him, 'Man, that is really a work of art.'" He wanted the men to be able to earn a little money for themselves or to send something to a loved one. But now all that was threatened.

Days later the 359 inmates from Camp F sat assembled at the prison arena as Warden Cain spoke. He explained the policy, as he had many times before. He also said, "I can explain it *to* you, but I can't understand it *for* you. You have to understand it for yourself." He turned to his security staff and told them in front of all the inmates never again to use the term "rat" to refer to a "good citizen" who was reporting wrongdoing. ("That's how we caught the three using drugs," he said afterward.) A good citizen had saved the hobby shop by identifying the perpetrators—and so the shop would be reopened.

"We crossed over that bump," Cain said later, "and we're on the road again—'whipping and spurring,' as the old cowboy said—to moral rehabilitation."

Slowly, some of the inmates are starting to get it. What "it" is, we will look at in more depth in the next chapter.

CHAPTER 4

MANUFACTURED HOPE

Imagine every morning waking up in prison, crawling out of a cot, brushing your teeth, putting on work clothes, and facing another monotonous day. Imagine hoping that during the course of this particular day, you have become eligible for parole—maybe not immediately but in a year or two. Imagine, then, working, eating, watching TV, or playing cards and eventually crawling back into the same cot—knowing as you fall asleep nothing has changed, nothing at all to even hint at the likelihood that you will eventually get out of this place. Now, repeat the same experience literally thousands of times, starting each day with a new dose of "manufactured hope"—and ending it crushed, as usual.

This is life in even the "best" of penal institutions—a breeding ground for despair, a dying by inches. And a despairing prisoner can be a dangerous prisoner, as Burl Cain recognized. Cain recognized something else: Prisoners are human beings.

Society, however, begs to differ. Society considers the men who populate prisons as pariahs. The first time someone becomes a "nonperson" is on the day of sentencing. The defendant has been found guilty, often after a lengthy and grueling trial. The law spells out what is appropriate, and the judge, or "sentencing authority," must rule by it. Sometimes, he or she can impose an extended sentence, adding to the term when it is evident that aggravating circumstances were present. These circumstances made the crime even worse than it needed to be. Yet even without receiving an extended term in prison, someone convicted of murder or a particularly violent felony achieves "nonperson" status when the judge pronounces the sentence. In Louisiana, second-degree murder, for which many states require a long but determinate sentence, often sends someone to prison for life. Angola—the state's only maximum-security penitentiary—receives anyone sentenced for forty years or longer.

The inmates who have been sentenced to life are the most severely affected. Their sentences never end; they cannot be paroled. Their only avenue to freedom is the rare pardon that the governor signs.

Such is the power of hope, though, that even a one-hundred-year sentence may not be onerous enough to squelch the deep-seated hope of an inmate that he may still leave Angola. For such men, the words "someday" take on extraordinary meaning. They cling to the hope of eventual release from prison even though they know, without doubt, that the sentence, if not cut short, barring a miracle, exceeds their natural life expectancy. To hang precariously on to such thin hope, inmates imagine achieving virtual immortality, walking out, free, someday when the last year of their sentence is complete.

In *The Shawshank Redemption,* the Morgan Freeman character, imprisoned for forty years or so and long since rehabilitated, is shown repeatedly going before his parole board and repeatedly being turned down with a "DENIED" stamp on the file. For many incarcerated in Louisiana, pardon is an equally elusive dream. The pardon board, appointed by the governor, has wide discretion in reviewing inmates' prison records and the crimes they committed before deciding whether to recommend parole.

Inmates serving life sentences without possibility of parole have only one extremely narrow way to win their freedom. They must turn to a pardon board, whose powers are as broad as those of the parole board. In the rare instances where an inmate wins a pardon recommendation, and the governor accepts it, he is not likely to be freed immediately. Instead, the governor will substitute a term of additional years that the inmate must serve before being eligible for parole consideration.

The parole/pardon process is meant to discourage inmates from thinking they may someday be free again. But—human nature being what it is—"manufactured hope" lives at Angola and in all prisons.

Certainly some criminals—some crimes—deserve harsh, lengthy sentences. They are applied to the worst of the worst to ensure that inmates who do horrible things in civilized society go to prison for many, many years or forever.

But the punishment that society inflicts on most violent criminals extends beyond the terms to which they are sentenced. Few citizens lose any sleep over what happens to those sentenced to prison—the "nonpersons".

And yet the application of long prison sentences is meant to have a harsh impact on defendants who are guilty. The people who put them away —the juries that recommend life without parole, the judges who impose the sentences—do not want to know what happens to them once they have left the courtroom and gone to prison. Only when someone sentenced to death is finally executed does society care to know that the ultimate punishment has been carried out. Then most people are content to read about the execution in a few paragraphs buried deep inside the daily newspaper.

The problem with this dehumanizing attitude and view of punishment is that criminals sent to prison for fifty years, seventy-five years, or even longer, even those who get life without the *possibility* of parole, are still very much alive—often with many years to live. They remain human beings no different in their needs, and often no different in their continuing desire to make something of themselves, from those who have sent them away. Without hope and without a will to achieve something worthwhile, despite what they have done, these inmates may well degenerate to acting no different than brutal animals. It is a condition that penal experts like Burl Cain recognize can be averted only when men achieve moral rehabilitation.

Cain says flatly: "Moral people are not criminals. That's why moral rehabilitation is the only true rehabilitation."

Moral rehabilitation means learning to live, peacefully and productively, in a prison community. It can be achieved, and is being achieved by an increasing number of inmates at Angola, but rarely unless a man makes his peace with God. Warden Cain has seen the wisdom of making it possible for the inmates housed at Angola, some for many decades, to reach out for that kind of moral rehabilitation. It is prudent to explore, then, how that has been accomplished by focusing on inmates who otherwise would be dying by inches as they live the rest of their lives in captivity.

New inmates arrive at Angola's front gate by bus, frightened and bewildered, clinging to hope, finally realizing this is where they will remain—a place that will only be as kind to them as they are good to it. The first person who meets the bus, along with security and classification staff, is an inmate minister, trained through the prison's college program. The inmate minister tells the new arrivals, "You can go with me and be involved in moral rehabilitation, or you can go with the predators. The choice is yours."

Usually the new inmates are scared, so they cast their lot with the inmate minister and moral rehabilitation. And, over time, they may learn to make their peace with Angola—a place they are unlikely ever to leave.

Burl Cain believes it takes up to ten years before most inmates accept that they probably are never going to be free again and begin to adjust to make the most of their prison surroundings. Some learn more quickly than others; some never learn and wind up confined to single cells, in virtual solitary, for years without end. The ones who make their peace with Angola get to work in the hobby shops, producing leather crafts for the rodeo. They learn trades, help others, or perhaps even have the opportunity to earn a college education and learn to become inmate ministers, prison lawyers, or teachers of literacy.

The choice is theirs. Or, as the warden is fond of saying, "Have it your way."

Yet the inmates are only part of the story. Those paid to keep the prison running also have their part to play, and it isn't easy. The situation in maximum-security prisons like Angola taxes the resources of the jailers charged with the responsibility, first and foremost, of keeping their inmates under lock and key. The public not only wants the criminals out of sight and mind. They can never escape and threaten society again. Much money is spent to construct safer, bigger, more awesome, escape-proof facilities.

Sometimes, though not often enough, the funds also are spent to compensate those who guard the inmates, protect them from each other, take care of them, and, finally, teach them to accept the life they will lead behind bars and high fences topped with rolling strands of razor-sharp wire. Accomplishing these tasks requires a level of professionalism from staff too often lacking ability or training in dealing with incarcerated men, staff who too often abuse their responsibilities and the human beings in their care.

Cain knows that society can ill afford to treat inmates as nonpersons. That has been tried in the past and it failed miserably. A hellishly operated prison puts inmates in grave danger, and it threatens the safety of those in charge. All efforts must be consumed maintaining the peace, which is a practical impossibility, short of ultimate repression, where the inmate populations outnumber even the best-staffed prison. The conditions in such environments are particularly horrible for the inmates who, no matter how hard they try to rise above it, eventually are diminished, bereft of any hope, dangerous to themselves and to everyone around them.

Burl Cain and his key staff are widely credited for making Angola into a peaceful, livable place, where inmates who desire to adapt and make something of themselves can do so.

But even the most progressive warden must rule with an iron fist. For Burl Cain, that means landing hard on those who fail to live by the rules. It also means extending, with an inviting, outstretched hand, privileges and opportunities to inmates who go along with his program and genuinely try to be "good citizens." Cain says—and people know he means it—that if anyone hurts him, that is, tries to disrupt the prison or harm anyone inside it, he will hurt them in return and, probably, inflict greater pain in the process. Despite the bravado of that statement, the philosophy, carried out judiciously, creates an atmosphere where the inmates respect the people who operate the prison because they know they won't be subjected to wanton cruelty or uneven, arbitrary treatment.

Cain also knows he and his staff cannot afford to be seen as weak or vacillating. Nor can they be seen as capricious or cruel. A warden whose prison is riddled by many unsuccessful escape attempts or who fails to prevent injury or even death to inmates or staff is likely to be fired. A warden who allows his staff to hurt inmates risks being subjected to a federal judge's oversight, the loss of his job, or worse.

On its surface, Angola is nothing more than a tough prison, where the state of Louisiana sends its most fearsome criminals. Cain and his staff win points by keeping the place under control, by ensuring no one hurts anyone else or tries to escape. But under the warden's leadership, Angola is becoming something more than simply a maximum-security penitentiary. It is becoming a community, just like any other community.

This community is no ordinary place. Men populate it who have done things that make many of them unsuitable to enjoy real freedom again. But in a strange twist of events, convicted criminals can come to Angola and start fresh. It's up to them. They can embrace the opportunity to put aside what got them committed to prison in the first place, and, depending on their willingness to conform and adapt, achieve a dream or aspiration, something they can view with pride as a real accomplishment. That is what the rodeo and craft shows are about, along with many other programs underway at Angola. That, too, is what moral rehabilitation is meant to achieve.

This is what "community" looks like at the end of a life.

Guests accompanying Warden Cain on a brief tour of Angola are privileged during their visit to witness the funeral of John Whitlock, number 111547, age sixty-seven, who became an inmate in 1987 after a judge sentenced him to life for murdering a man in 1983. Whitlock made the most of his situation, rising to the status of Class A trustee, the highest level that one can achieve as an inmate. He got paid at a rate of twenty cents an hour, rather than the four cents an hour that other inmates receive. He also earned a certain measure of freedom inside Angola, not to mention the respect and love of others around him.

Johnny Whitlock knew he was dying; he just didn't know when. The cancer had spread, and he was confined to the prison's hospice area where inmate friends could visit and comfort him. There also were inmate hospice volunteers to ease his pain. Death was coming soon, and time was running out. Whitlock did not have to stare into the worried faces of those who cared for him to understand that. He was an easy terminal patient, asking for very little as he lay on his deathbed.

He did make two final requests—one easy to satisfy, the other a bit odd and definitely more difficult to arrange. First, because he had no family, Johnny wanted to be buried in the prison cemetery, Point Lookout 2. That was easy to grant. Second, he asked that the two horses that would pull his casket to the graveyard in an antique, black, glass-sided funeral hearse wagon be of different colors, a black one and a white one. Johnny, his friends said with admiration, had never been a man to consider others of greater or lesser value on the basis of their race. All men were equal in his sight, and the men who shared dormitory space with him appreciated that so much. His friends, both white and African-American, would line up behind the old hearse to transport his casket to the grave site.

Having horses of different colors to draw the hearse wagon was something else altogether. In keeping with his views on racial equality, John whispered to his caregivers that it would be most fitting if a black and a white horse—both huge Percherons, easily as large as the Budweiser Clydesdales—could be teamed together to draw the hearse to the grave-yard. That was not something that was usually allowed. The horses paired for the prison rodeo and other occasions are accustomed to working in teams of blacks or whites, not mixed as Johnny requested.

There was some concern that a mixed team would resist the unusual arrangement, that the different-colored Percherons would strain mightily at being yoked side by side, that one of them would head one way, and the other would refuse to follow. The last thing anyone wanted during a solemn funeral was to have to corral a runaway team of gigantic steeds with the funeral hearse careering off the road. Yet out of respect for Johnny Whitlock, the men who managed the teams agreed to give it a try.

It was a sunny afternoon, the sweltering heat not all that unusual for this time of year, on the first of November, when the group of inmates, Johnny's friends and hospice attendants, settled in behind the old hearse. Lloyd Bone, "Bones" to his friends, was mounted high in a seat atop the hearse, awaiting the signal to send the Percherons down the road to the cemetery. Bones was resplendent in a black tuxedo, black high-top hat, and shiny black shoes. He sat perfectly still, reins held loosely in his hands, seemingly sure that he could control the giant Percherons in front of him.

When the signal was given, the driver firmly applied the reins to the horses' rumps. Bedecked with red ribbons in their manes and outfitted in black gear, the two horses, black and white, came down the narrow road together, with nary a fuss, as though they had done this all their existence. The hearse moved slowly, almost majestically, the horses steady and in tan-dem, their slow clip-clop, clip-clop measured and precise. The procession made its way from an inmate park, where the mourners had gathered, to the cemetery, less than a quarter mile away.

A small crowd had already gathered at the grave site. Three inmates had freshly dug it by hand, put up a white tent covering, and rolled out grass-colored mats over the large mounds of earth that they had excavated on each side of the grave. It was a professional job, done with great care.

Only a sudden change in the weather could spoil the scene. And that was about to happen. In the distance, onlookers could see dark, swirling clouds rapidly drawing near. Rain, a steady, piercing drizzle, suddenly pelted the unprotected mourners as the horse-drawn hearse arrived at the site. Someone opened an umbrella, and, for a moment, it appeared as though one horse would try to bolt, its huge frame swaying back and forth, its hooves pawing the ground nervously. But Bones kept the team under control, and the pallbearers quickly unloaded the precious cargo.

The men carrying the casket slid it onto thin wooden rails over the hole. Inmates had lovingly made the dark wooden coffin, stained and varnished, a wooden cross atop its lid. Long, wooden pole handles enabled the pallbearers to position the casket just so. Then they flanked the grave site. Other mourners huddled together tightly around them, as many as could fit under the tent. Just then, as the service commenced, the rain let up as quickly as it had begun and a warm sun emerged to dry out everyone.

"We're here to say good-bye to our good friend, Johnny, to remember what he stood for, to send him on his way," the inmate preacher began. He opened to a passage in his well-weathered Bible and quoted generously from the verses. Johnny, the preacher said, had placed his faith in Jesus, and he was now in the arms of his Savior. Soon two elderly men took turns saluting their departed friend—"he never let me down," said one. Then another inmate, an American Indian, strummed his guitar softly as he sang the opening verse of "Amazing Grace"—Johnny requested only one song, "Amazing Grace," sung by one singer, the Native American.

Finally, the pallbearers lowered the casket into the grave. Someone tossed Johnny's blue cap onto the casket, a cherished cap he always wore, to accompany him to his final resting place. Others pulled a few bright red carnations from a funereal wreath placed at one end of the grave and tossed them on top of the box in a final salute. A few scooped up handfuls of dirt to scatter over the casket as the grave diggers approached to begin shoveling the mounds of earth into the hole.

With that Johnny Whitlock was laid to rest.

In a beautifully crafted casket borne in an antique hearse by white and black horses, with his friends there to shed tears as they said good-bye, Johnny got what he sought throughout his years in prison—a measure of dignity and respect. One visitor remarked that there are free people who die and do not receive the same degree of attention, love, or care at their funerals.

Johnny's funeral was a far cry from the way things used to be at Angola, when, as the warden said, the attitude was "put them in and cover it up." Some old-timers still recall the time when inmates who died were buried in makeshift cardboard caskets purchased cheaply from a local casket supplier. They remember the day when an inmate's body fell through the bottom of a rain-sodden cardboard box just as the pallbearers positioned it over the grave. They describe the shock of seeing the inmate's body tumble into the hole, and the pallbearers simply letting go of the crumpled cardboard mess so that it collapsed on top of the corpse, the whole mess unceremoniously obscured by dirt.

"This has to change," Cain declared. Inmate preachers could officiate at the funerals, he said; inmate carpenters could build the caskets. One master carpenter, nicknamed "Redwine," declared, "I'm gonna make them good—paint and polish each one 'cause I don't know which one will be mine." Redwine has since died and was buried in one of "his" coffins.

The Angola of the past, where men went to bed at night not knowing whether they would see dawn or die violently at the hands of other inmates, where prisoners struggled to survive in an atmosphere of cruelty and neglect, where the strong lorded over the weak, where guards were at best indifferent and at worst brutal—that Angola has largely vanished.

CHAPTER 5

WHAT IT FEELS LIKE

When an inmate arrives at Angola, particularly when he has been sentenced to life without the possibility of parole, he often loses much more than his freedom. As the days, weeks, months, and years in prison pile up, the people in his life fall away. Many men already arrive at Angola with little family support. The environment into which they grew up may well have contributed to or triggered the events that resulted in their convictions. But other inmates enter Angola with obvious support systems on the outside. They are married, and they may have children. They have mothers and fathers, brothers and sisters, aunts, uncles, cousins, and even nieces and nephews—large extended families. In the beginning, they pledge to be there for the inmate. They show up for his trial. They promise to visit, write letters. But as time stretches on, these promises often prove hollow.

Distant relatives tend to drift away from the get-go. But a man expects his wife, if he has one, kids, if he has them, and certainly his parents to stick by him forever. The first real blow comes when the inmate's wife sends him the inevitable "Dear John" letter. The marriage isn't sup-posed to end like this, and he wonders why, even though to an outsider the reason is crystal clear.

When the inmate first arrived at Angola, his spouse was there, faith-fully, twice a month. They spent precious time together, four hours a visit at most, as physically close as they could get in public in the visitors' room, pledging their love and loyalty. (Angola does not permit conjugal visits.) He expected, naively, that she would always be there, in sickness and in health and, by extension, in prison as well.

Then the visits began to dwindle. She explained that it was too expensive to travel to Angola every couple of weeks. Now the discussions they had in the noisy visitors' room seemed to focus more on the problems she was having paying bills and disciplining the kids, and noticeably less on how much she missed him and longed for the day they could be to-gether again. Of course, the romance was beginning to fade. They had vir-tually no physical intimacy, nor was it permissible or in any way possible under these visitation conditions. Both were frustrated, but while she had an out, he did not. Yet he kept telling her that someday they would live and love together once again even though, deep down, he knew better.

Now the wife only showed up once a month, and she made it clear that each trip was an exhausting ordeal. She rarely accepted his collect calls, complaining that her tight household budget simply didn't have room in it for expensive, long-distance phone bills. When he did see her, less and less frequently, it dawned on the inmate that the woman sitting across the table from him was becoming a virtual stranger.

What's more, the times they spent during these visits were becom-ing increasingly dissatisfying. They would argue, and she would accuse him of abandoning her. Each time, after she left, he would return to his dormitory or cell wondering where all of this was headed. He wistfully twirled the wedding ring on his finger and hoped against hope that things would be better the next time she showed up. They never were. The inmate began to entertain thoughts of escaping from this place. (That's why Burl Cain requires an inmate be at Angola for ten years before being eligible to become a trustee; those first years are when he's most likely to try to get out.)

Finally she wrote, and he would never forget this most devastating letter. No matter how carefully she chose the words or tried to soften the blow, the message struck him harder than anything else he had experienced since arriving at Angola. Without fail, the simple, declarative sentence "I'm filing for a divorce" was the line that rattled him the most, that echoed through his head as he wept in the dark, that caused him to pull the blanket high over his head so no one would see him crying.

Once an inmate had only nine days left to serve his time. His wife told him, "You can't come home. I have another man." The inmate climbed the fence, went home, and attempted murder.

With his wife gone from his life, it became harder for the inmate's children to come on visitors' day. Sometimes their grandmother—his mama—brought them. And sometimes the daughters remained loyal while the sons drifted away.

By the time they were old enough to make it to Angola on their own, they no longer had any interest in seeing the old man. He was locked up, after all, and had no input into their lives—what useful advice could he give? He didn't even have a few dollars he could share so they could have a good time on the weekend. Besides, what teenager would want friends to know that Dad was a "con" sentenced to prison for life?

The inmate discovered that the end of any contact with his children was even harder to accept than seeing his wife bail out on him. The kids were his flesh and blood, his future—the only potential decent legacy he had left behind when he entered Angola. And now they often wouldn't answer his letters or moved without telling him where they were going. In short, it soon became devastatingly apparent they wanted nothing to do with him.

But he still had his parents, and he knew he could count on them. They continued to visit regularly, like clockwork. They might not have the money to travel often. The trips might occur once a month, or maybe once every other month, or maybe even less frequently than that, depending on their physical frailties and financial circumstances. Regardless, when the appointed day arrived, the inmate could enter the visitation area knowing his mother and father would already be there expectantly in the visitors' room. They were always happy to see him, hugging him tightly, planting kisses on his cheeks, even weeping as they told him how much they still loved him.

Then one day, the first dreaded message came from the outside. The prison chaplain and an inmate minister sat down with the prisoner in a private place. There's been a death in your family, they told him. In all probability the deceased parent was the inmate's father, a man grown old too soon as he struggled to cope with the knowledge that his son had killed or committed some other horrible crime. His father may well have died with a broken heart, believing he had failed his son, that if he had done what was right, his flesh and blood would not be languishing in prison.

The inmate minister stayed with the prisoner to comfort and counsel as needed, but the loss still hurt deeply. A few days later the inmate got to make a rare, quick trip to his hometown, given permission to attend his dead parent's funeral (unless he was on Death Row or had a bad disciplinary record). He could not go alone. The prison escorted him there, monitoring his every move. Only if he was a trustee, did the inmate get to make the trip in street clothes, and enter the funeral home or church without handcuffs or leg irons, but still in a leg brace to keep him from running. If he were a trustee, two correctional officers, one armed and one not, were on hand, staying in the background but remaining watchful as the prisoner mingled with other family members.

But if he was simply an ordinary inmate, he might have nothing better to wear than his typical prison outfit—a white or gray T-shirt, blue jeans, and sneakers. His wrists and ankles might be bound to prevent an escape attempt. His guard would never leave his side until he returned to prison.

Worst of all, on the day he was there to witness the burial of his parent, the inmate might have to endure awkward and condemning stares of other guests. He might even see them casting critical glances in his direction and overhear them whispering, yet loud enough for him to hear, that his criminal act had driven his father to an early death. That hurt the most.

Then finally, there came a second awful message. This time, the inmate's remaining parent was gone, and now he was alone, with no one on the outside who still cared about him or his circumstances. The second message hit him particularly hard if the last parent to die was his mother. Burl Cain says, "No one loves you like your mama. No one can replace her when she's gone." Even though the inmate's mother may have lived for a long time, he still could not let go. For days or even weeks, he might break out in sobs at the most inappropriate times.

The inmate could not help but cry as he recalled how his mother never criticized him for what he had done, always sent him a Christmas present, always mailed a birthday card with money inside. He longed to have her cradle his face in her hands on visitors' day. Most of all, the inmate would weep when he remembered that, to her, he was always "my beloved son."

"Your mama is always there for you," Cain says, reflecting on the impact that mothers play in prisoners' lives. "She always wants the best for you. She wants to know that you are doing all right in prison. And when everyone else abandons you, she stands by, no matter what you have done, no matter how despicable was the act that you committed. She is also a victim."

Even after a man has been sentenced to death for a horrific crime that has caused society to label him a monster, his mother will hug him on Death Row and hold him tightly, one last time, as he awaits his execution.

The shredding of relationships with those an inmate has loved and sees depart from him while he is in prison can destroy whatever spark of kindness and compassion he might have retained when he first arrived at Angola. These were emotions he hid deep inside, afraid to display around other prisoners who might see his soft side as a sign of weakness to be exploited. Yet they could surface on visiting day when he saw smiles from his family as he entered the recreation room to meet with them.

But when the tenuous connections to the outside world eventually snapped for good, the inmate turned inward—and turned bitter. He might even begin to resent others around him who still had family members seeing them on visiting days, sending letters that they read over and over again, making telephone calls that they were willing to accept. Cain and his staff encourage letter writing over phone calls because sending a letter is cheaper and, more important, it gives family members something to hold on and pass around.

Burl Cain has taken risks to open up the prison so prisoners can continue to experience links to a world that mostly wants to forget that they exist.

On a recent fall Sunday, Angola hosted an all-day program where a couple of hundred inmates invited their children to join them in a more natural, relaxed atmosphere than what exists typically around a small table in a noisy, packed visitors' room.

The prison's chaplain, Robert Toney, got the idea from Scottie Barnes, a woman whose dad had been in prison. She remembered how she never got to hold her father until he was released. He died shortly thereafter.

On that fall Sunday the fathers and their children enjoyed each other's company in a large outdoor recreational area, with tents to shade them, games and recreational equipment to entertain them, and food and beverages to provide the energy for an entire day of fun. There were clowns, snow cones, cotton candy, a giant slide to tumble down. For some of the men, this was the first time in months—if not years—that they had had any real opportunity to be with their offspring. They talked with them, held them tight, and tried to reinstill an abiding love in sons and daughters who had not had that kind of attention from their fathers since they went to prison. Most of all, some of the men finally had the chance to say they were sorry for abandoning their kids.

The event was a huge success. Photos of tearful yet smiling dads and kids, playing together and enjoying one another's company, told an upbeat, emotional story far more eloquently than a thousand words could ever do.

One inmate, seeing his three teenage daughters for the first time in years, had the opportunity to tell them about Christ. The inmate had committed his life to Christ just that day. The three daughters were among ten children of prisoners who attended summer camp at Word of Life Ministries in Schroon Lake, in upstate New York. The proud inmate still has a newspaper clipping of the photo showing him surrounded by those three attractive young women.

"We couldn't do it without church support," says Cain. "Some churches provided buses to pick up children. There was tremendous involvement."

Yet not everyone was pleased that Angola put on this special occasion.

"My son was killed by one of your convicts, and he'll never get to see his boys again," wrote one mother in a letter to Cain. "I resent the fact that his killer gets to play with his kids."

While understanding her anger, the warden sees something else, something most of us don't think about. "It wasn't simply that we gave a few inmates a special opportunity to see their children. Those kids are victims too. They don't deserve to be without fathers, to face a difficult growing-up experience without a dad to support them. Perhaps by strengthening what remains of a fragile bond between the dads and their kids, we can keep some in the next generation from repeating the mistake of the fathers. We are trying to break the cycle.

"I don't believe I am required to punish the kids by depriving them of an opportunity to see their dads on an occasion like the one we held in the fall. They already are being punished enough by not being allowed to see their dads except on visiting days. This event—which we plan to carry out again—sent a message to our men too, that we're not here to add to their misery or to isolate them from families they are desperate to maintain even as they serve long or life sentences."

In a place like Angola, where the majority of the inmates are imprisoned for life without any possibility of parole, the mind-sets of the men are of paramount concern to the warden and his staff. As we have seen, prisoners who cannot adjust become even more embittered when supposedly loving family members abandon them. They become likely candidates to channel hostile energies in ways that threaten the safety of others.

Burl Cain's solution, in part, has been to open up Angola to the outside world, to allow all types of groups to work with inmates, to show free people that the men imprisoned there are not all predators.

The "in-reach" occurs in many ways. Taking the place of the gangs that terrorize—and run—so many of the nation's prisons are thirty inmate clubs, operated by organizations like Toastmasters of America and the Dale Carnegie Institute, and other outside religious groups. An extensive college program run by the New Orleans Baptist Theological Seminary allows inmates to graduate with degrees in pastoral studies, theology, and general studies. Those going through the program can become inmate ministers, inmate lawyers, or literacy teachers—important in a community where the average education level is fifth grade. (Cain would like to see it raised to eighth grade.) Bible reading is an important part of creating a positive culture at Angola. The Sharon Miceli Long Fund, named in memory of the warden's wife's sister, provides picture Bibles to inmates through the efforts of the First Presbyterian Church of Baton Rouge. Meanwhile, as literacy levels rise, prisoners will be able to "graduate" to more advanced versions.

And the biggest "in-reach" of all is the Angola Prison Rodeo, an annual event that attracts thousands of outsiders to the prison to see "The Wildest Show in the South."

Angola has held a rodeo for more than forty years. It started as a "behind the barn" sort of event, initiated by a former prisoner known as Cadillac Jack Favor. But it has blossomed into a huge event in recent years, attracting as many as ten thousand visitors each day during a weekend in April and every Sunday in October. The action takes place in Angola's all-purpose arena, on a special field "padded" with tilled, fertile dark brown earth, surrounded by a large, sturdy oval grandstand built by inmates for nine thousand spectators. (Cain points out that no taxpayer dollars were used in construction of the arena, which has hosted, among other luminaries, Joyce Meyer, the Brooklyn Tabernacle Choir, Chuck Colson, Aaron Neville, and Harry Connick Jr.. A $500,000 donation from the Pennington Foundation paid the entire cost of the material, and the inmates provided the labor.)

Once inside the area where the rodeo is held, visitors seem to forget that the grounds are encircled by a high, barbed wire-crowned fence. They seem to minimize the inconvenience of having to pass by correctional officers on the lookout for contraband. Nor do they seem concerned that they are rubbing shoulders with some men who have committed violent crimes. No ominous signs warn against inappropriate interactions between the inmates and the spectators. The corrections staff keeps a low, but diligent, profile. The atmosphere of openness and spontaneity is comparable to what one might find at any popular sporting event. Spectators range in age from toddlers in strollers to old-timers, some of whom have been coming to the rodeo for many years. Visitors are likely to encounter pleasant, casually dressed men who seem no different than they are—open, smiling, and happy to greet the public attending the event.

Angola's rodeo is the most ambitious effort of all to show society that in many respects inmates harbor the same desires to win respect and achieve success as anyone else. At the same time, the rodeo allows many of the prison's inmates to see that the barrier separating them from society is not impenetrable. Though they may never again live as free people, they can at least connect with the outside world a few times a year.

Professionals from a touring rodeo company manage the event, but every rider in every event is a rank amateur who almost certainly has never before come into contact with snorting, bucking horses or frenzied bulls before arriving at Angola. The pros give participants a few helpful clues—

more than simply "run like the wind when a bull is chasing you"—and a briefing before they take on a wild animal. Most important, they help the inmates put on safety chest padding to protect them when they fall or happen to sustain an angry animal's kick as they roll onto the ground.

The events include "convict poker" in which four men sit gingerly around a table as a bull approaches, then charges them. The last man still in his chair wins. There is also something called "guts and glory," and another event where inmates try to milk a wild cow. Inmates also play "buddy pickup," where one man on horseback gallops across the outdoor arena to pick up a second inmate atop a barrel and then returns as fast as he can to the starting point.

Is the rodeo stacked against the inmates? One critic has likened it to a Roman gladiator contest, claiming that the inmates are not adequately prepared for events pitting them against dangerous animals. And certainly the risk of serious injury—or worse—rides in with any rodeo. But none of the inmates is forced to participate; the men are all willing volunteers. Nor does anyone promote the show as a place where spectators with bloodlust can see someone get hurt. Media from as far as Britain, Sweden, Australia, the Netherlands, Japan, and Belgium come and cover the event. When they asked the warden about the danger to the men, he replied, "This is no different from the running of the bulls in Spain. At least here we have a fence they can climb over to get away."

The rodeo is a big moneymaker for Angola, providing funds for inmate programs and building projects such as chapels. In addition, it is a major source of spending money for inmates who participate in the events or sell crafts at a show that is becoming a huge side event during the rodeo. Many inmates offer homemade crafts, toys, and artwork at the show, and many spectators come for the day even if they cannot see the rodeo. They take leisurely strolls throughout the craft area, purchasing items on sale and gorging themselves on piping bowls of crawdad stew and other Louisiana delicacies made by inmate cooks and the employee recreation committee.

Most of Angola's camps include hobby shops where men work for months building furniture, composing artwork, making leather goods, and hammering out metal decorative jewelry and belt buckles for sale during the rodeo. For these amateur artisans, the craft show is a time to sell their wares to the public and earn money for their prison accounts. It is possible for a man to make several hundred dollars, most of which he can put into his account for personal use or to purchase more supplies to produce goods for the next rodeo. While inmates are not allowed to have cash, Angola provides a banking system, whereby inmates can make withdrawals out of their accounts on a computer, even, Cain says, to have the "dignity of being able to pay for a meal for his family" when they visit. Inmates also pay taxes on their show earnings.

But "The Wildest Show in the South" is much more than simply a moneymaker for the prison and its inmates. You can't place a dollar figure on the value of the opportunity it offers to inmates—men who may be completely alone in the world—to bask in the glow of praise from outsiders. It is also an opportunity for the taxpaying public to see a clean, well-maintained prison, to see that the prison is, as Cain puts it, "a place where moral rehabilitation is taking place and their tax dollars are well spent."

And they could see Johnny Brooks in action.

Brooks, a slim black man with a gaping smile and a jaunty appearance in his cowboy outfit, was for years the virtual king of the "The Wildest Show in the South," an inmate who consistently won more rodeo events than anyone else. The producers featured him in a network television program focusing on the rodeo, and he appeared on camera smiling broadly as he explained what the event meant to him. He didn't say so in so many words, but the gist of his message was clear.

Brooks's goal to be Angola's top rider at the rodeo was important for more than the small cash awards he received or the grudging respect that other inmates bestowed on him. He thoroughly enjoyed the attention from the crowd in the grandstand. It was intoxicating for Brooks to hear the cheers when he took a series of jolts sure to rattle the man's very frame, and when he would not let loose of the slippery reins that he held, ever so tightly, to avoid being hurled roughly to the ground.

His family had long since deserted him, but he overcame the loneliness by making friends among other inmates, by reconciling himself to the fact he was paying a necessary price for carrying out a horrible deed years ago, when he was a young man out of control. He knew that meant he would never leave Angola alive. So he vowed to make the best of his time in this place. He would show others, and indeed the world if he could, that Johnny Brooks was more than a killer.

So he threw himself into the rodeo. Though he might not ever see a family visitor on the weekends, he would still have something to hang on to, a link to a sliver of the world that seemed to appreciate his skills as a cowboy. He was quite the sight, in his black, wide-brimmed hat, in the bright green chaps, and matching vest that he made in the hobby shop. (The last two items are now on display at Angola's museum.) As he settled atop a horse or a snorting bull inside a chute, waiting his turn to ride, Brooks could inhale the scent of the wild animal beneath him. He could sense the surge of adrenaline building to a crescendo within him, wipe the sweat rolling off his face with a colorful bandanna, and anticipate how good it would be to land in that soft arena dirt after abandoning his mount.

But it was the crowd's approval, a loud roar that gave Johnny an exhilarating rush more than enough to carry him on to the next rodeo. It was a kind of success he had never known before. The free people wanted him to remain aboard a frenzied animal long enough to score points. They rooted hard as he hung on while a furious, bucking animal tried to shed him from its back, then hurl him into space and trample him beneath its heavy hoofs.

Brooks would beat the animal at its game, as he often did. He would release his hold and depart to the soft dirt only when he was good and ready. He would tumble from the horse or bull without getting hurt. Then he would quickly spring up from the dirt that had cushioned his fall. He would run over to where his black cowboy hat had fallen and quickly replace it on his head, just so, to give him that jaunty, cowboy appearance.

Then he would brush off the dirt clinging to his chaps, gesture appreciatively with a tip of his hat, and stroll out of the arena as the spirited animal he had defeated finally gave up leaping and kicking.

One day, in October 1999, Johnny Brooks, the cowboy king, Angola's No. 86002, died. His unexpected death at the age of forty-five occurred in the middle of a week when he was steeling himself once again for the challenge of a Sunday rodeo. Perhaps he was contemplating how better to adjust his grip on a bucking bronco or envisioning that anticipated rush of victory. As he stood beside Assistant Warden Darrel Vannoy's truck, Brooks swooned and fell to the ground. Other inmates, as well as Warden Vannoy, tried in vain to revive him. The rodeo committee dedicated the remaining weeks of the annual event to Brooks who went down harder, fatally, from a massive coronary attack than any agitated bull could have ever thrown him.

Warden Cain granted a request that Johnny had shared often with him and others. The king of Angola's cowboys wanted to be buried under the branches of a large black walnut tree, the only tree bordering one of two inmate cemeteries, known as Point Lookout 2. The cemetery is a pleasant place where many of the prison's inmates have been laid to rest, and many more are sure to follow.

Johnny Brooks had a spectacular funeral. Inmate Bones drove the hearse. The Angola Rough Riders, mounted behind, carried the flag. The funeral was well attended by inmates and staff. His rodeo buddies lowered Brooks's casket into a freshly dug grave just beyond that solitary tree. For now, he is separated from other inmate graves, which are in rows at one end of the cemetery, a considerable distance from his grave site. But it will not always be that way. Someday the gap will close between his resting place and those of an increasing number of men who die after spending most of their lives at Angola.

Angola, a peaceful prison community for the living, where Johnny Brooks made his home for many years, is also being transformed into the somber community of crosses over the graves of the dead.

Visitors to Lookout Point 2 invariably make their way to the solitary concrete cross under which Brooks is interred. They sometimes inquire about the black cowboy hat attached to its top. The well-worn hat remains as a sort of sentry guarding his grave. Yet that will not always be so. Someday it, like its owner, will be gone. The hat already has lost part of its brim to the elements. It is ever so slowly disintegrating, a reluctant victim, like Brooks himself, to the inexorability of an environment beyond its control. But to this day some of the inmates say, "When the eagle flies overhead, that's Johnny Brooks."

Some inmates at Angola try to maintain a connection with the outside world another way. Some of them discover love after they arrive in prison, meeting women who for various reasons are attracted to them and find the bonds of matrimony to a lifer alluring to embrace. These relationships, in so many respects artificial at best, often begin with an introduction during a weekend visitation arranged by another inmate's female friend. Then follow brief, breathless phone calls and romantic letters and cards. (Pen pal relationships are discouraged, however, because of the risk of scams from such practices.)

Soon both parties, smitten, are discussing marriage, avoiding for the most part the obvious issues that dominate any union, particularly the fact that the inmate and his spouse-to-be may never enjoy conjugal rights, much less any real, long-term emotional intimacy.

The warden and his staff try to discourage such arrangements, knowing from sad experience that virtually none of these hasty marriages last. But the prison administration has no legal right to block an inmate from marrying, and so, on occasion, some men exchange vows with the women who have promised to stick by them, thick and thin. At these marriage ceremonies, other envious inmates may be in attendance. They, too, long to connect to eligible women on the outside, somehow to share companionship, however strained, with someone they believe they love and who loves them in return.

These are contrived arrangements, although it seems certain that neither the inmate nor his new wife regard them as such. Think about the conditions of these prison weddings, if you will. There will be no consummation of the marriage. Instead, physical intimacy is limited to a kiss or two, and a long embrace, after the vows have been exchanged, and there is a brief wedding reception in the visitors' room or prison chapel.

Then the inmate must return to his cell or dorm, and his wife goes back to her home. Their contacts after that are restricted weekly visits, letters, and phone calls, collect from him—the prison allows no outside calls to reach inmates.

From the very beginning, these marriages are on thin ice because there is little beyond the marriage license that the inmate and his beloved each signed. The couples cannot ever live together. The brief opportunities during visitation are limited to a kiss or two and a hug. The married inmates' behavior is closely monitored. The couples huddle together, forced to talk softly, sharing romantic words, in the crowded visitors' area. They strive in vain for precious privacy around a hard, metal table where someone else may have landed as well.

Then, too, they will never have the opportunity to grow in their marital bonds, to experience the highs of matrimony, let alone figure out ways to overcome the ordinary trials of any newlywed couples. Nor, for that matter, can they ever make realistic plans for the future. Some say, tongue in cheek, that a marriage to an inmate serving life allows a woman to enjoy the best of marriage. She has no obligations to fulfill him sexually, and she does not have to pick up after him when he's sloppy. The inmate gains, at least superficially, an anchor from the outside, someone he can write to, talk with, and occasionally hug and kiss. But he is frustrated, knowing he will never have the opportunity to make love to his wife or hold her close throughout the long night.

Inevitably, the illusory nature of this kind of romance and marriage wears off, and the wife, particularly, begins to realize the relationship to which she has committed herself is no relationship at all.

Then, inevitably as well, comes the day when she writes a "Dear John" letter. At that point, the cycle of an inmate's loneliness begins anew.

Someone at Angola has to pick up the pieces of a life that has been broken and shattered once again.

It gets worse at Christmas.

At Christmastime inmates at Angola ache more deeply to be free, to see their families, if they still have them—in short, to try and escape. In the Christmas season, family relationships fractured by incarceration become magnified and the men trying desperately to hang on to them pine for far-away loved ones. Like the free people who find the holidays depressing, not exhilarating, inmates can plunge into a deep melancholy and begin to go down potentially destructive mental paths. Warden Cain and his staff know that escape attempts—not all that commonplace the rest of the year—rise during the winter holidays.

Their answer, in addition to ensuring the security team is particularly vigilant, is to make the prison brighter than usual, with seasonal firs, Yule decorations, and multicolored lights springing up throughout the facility, and particularly in the prison camps. Groups that work with inmates are encouraged to be on the grounds during the holidays, and church choirs serenade with joyous carols and solemn hymns. Few efforts are spared to boost inmate spirits. For all that, some inmates still chafe at the thought of spending yet another Christmas behind bars, with all-too-brief weekend contact with their wives, children, or parents to encourage them. The prison's inmate missionaries circulate openly, inviting men distressed by their surroundings or depressed at the thought of not being with their families during the holidays to share their heartache.

But Cain and his team are limited in what they can do to spread holiday cheer in a maximum-security penitentiary where no inmates are ever likely to go home to celebrate any special occasion with families. Only so much can be done to alleviate the emotional lows during what should be a joyous occasion. In the end, the inmates considering an attempt to bolt still must keep in mind, without fail, that Angola's chase team will pursue them, relentlessly, until it tracks them down. The inmates must know that if they try to escape, real tragedy awaits. They may somehow get hurt or even killed during the attempt. They will be caught. It is not a warning; the warden pledges that no one will remain free after escaping.

The staff does not have to threaten to use force to recapture fleeing prisoners. At Angola, there are no idle threats, only sure reactions—pursuit by armed guards and tireless bloodhounds. Besides, the rugged, treacherous hills leading to St. Francisville, the other hostile natural surroundings, particularly the swift currents of the Mississippi River, are enough to discourage all but the most foolhardy.

The staff itself stands down a bit when the holidays finally pass, relieved that January has rolled around again, knowing that the men who had thoughts of escape abandoned them after all—and are still there as another year dawns.

CHAPTER 6

SOULS
BEHIND BARS

Some prisoners at Angola won't change. Not of their own accord. They'll remain soulless predators—unless something changes in their lives. They come to prison angry and determined not to cooperate any more than they must. They figure that if the world has rejected them, they will reject anything the world offers, even some opportunities in prison that may make an endless existence a bit more tolerable.

How do you even begin to reach these bitter, discarded human fragments?

Burl Cain believes there is one answer, one way to reach the offenders and convert them into men who genuinely seek to make something of themselves in prison. He believes there must be a true conversion —deep inside, touching an inmate's very soul, that secret place where virtually no man can fool himself. The warden believes moral rehabilitation must take place in order for an inmate to lift himself beyond the jungle atmosphere that too often can smother a prison.

Cain is committed to not only encouraging his inmates to search within themselves for the answers that lead to moral rehabilitation but also to wiping out, as nearly as possible, the environment that allows the predators to survive. It is a two-handed approach, delicately balanced. To the men who seek to rehabilitate themselves while serving long or life sentences, Burl Cain offers, as we have seen, educational programs, seminary training, clubs, hobbies, and crafts, even occasional trips outside Angola—in short, a measure of freedom even during incarceration. However, unless a man changes his ways, there is hard, tedious work in the fields, extended lockdown, and virtually no opportunity to attain any meaningful existence at Angola. But says Cain, "There is always light at the end of the tunnel for any man to change."

A man who breaks the rules and hurts others will find himself alone, inside a narrow cell with little to occupy his time. He will stay there for as long as it takes to show that he wants to act responsibly. It is up to him.

But if he gives it a chance . . .

Every weekday, more than one hundred men crowd into classrooms in a prison building at Angola to study the Bible and take courses that will enable them to serve as inmate missionaries. The New Orleans Baptist Theological Seminary operates the extension school at the prison. It is open to inmates of all faiths whose applications indicate they are likely to be successful in a rigorous, college-level program, accredited just the same as Louisiana State University.

The extension center began in September 1995. There were sixteen inmates in the first graduating class, seventeen in the second class, and thirty-five in the third. More than one hundred inmates are currently enrolled, with sixty-six graduating in May 2005. One notable statistic in extension seminary literature is that in one year, inmate ministers baptized one hundred and fifty inmates. They also averaged fifteen thousand evangelistic contacts a month.

Another two hundred and sixty inmates are enrolled in a certification program the seminary operates to teach men who do not qualify academically for the degree program. (Many inmates at Angola do not have a high school education or the equivalent. Improving literacy rates is an important goal of the staff's effort to change the prison environment.) Inmate students in the seminary must have a high school diploma or its equivalent. They must obtain letters of recommendation from someone in a pastor's role at Angola, saying they would be suitable to serve as inmate missionaries. They must explain in writing why they want to attend, and they must submit to an interview and probing questions about their motivation. They also must have completed the "Experiencing God" course, a practical, intense Bible study that millions across the globe have completed. The course teaches how to achieve a close relationship with God by adopting spiritual disciplines into daily life. Burl Cain himself has taken the course and found it to be life changing. It was his church group that sponsored the first study groups at Angola in April 1995.

Before anyone can be accepted into the seminary, there is one final hurdle. A committee of assistant wardens must review the application and evaluate the inmate's suitability based on how he has acclimated to prison life. Someone who has racked up infractions is unlikely to be approved for the program. Yet if the staff sees the spark of redemption of a man's conduct, he may still have the opportunity to attend.

Those enrolled in the seminary consider it their full-time prison jobs. They study and take tests. They are expected to carry what they learn into the prison's living areas, to help men around them achieve the aspirations of "Experiencing God." It is possible for an inmate to finish the four-year program—129 classroom hours—on schedule. Some, however, get into trouble elsewhere in the prison and are disciplined by removing them from the seminary. That is not always a permanent expulsion; they eventually can reapply after completing whatever requirements were imposed for their misconduct and by demonstrating they will abide by the prison's rules without fail.

Not every man who has finished seminary at Angola always had a sterling record as an inmate—as Jesse Deters's story demonstrates.

The people who knew him considered Jesse Deters to be incorrigible when he committed the aggravated rape that got him sent to Angola. He had also committed murder in Texas. For many years, Deters fought the prison system and was considered a troublemaker. Then, almost miraculously, he changed and was accepted to work as a clerk on the seminary staff. The program director, Dr. John Robson, said Deters became the "most doctrinally sound" member of his staff, someone "dedicated and gifted," who taught in a certificate program for inmates who could not meet the seminary's academic standards.

At the age of fifty-five, Deters died suddenly of a heart attack. "He'll be missed," Robson said of the inmate. Those who attended his funeral were astounded. Believing that Deters had never changed, they heard not what the man had been but instead they heard what he had become—a positive force in the twilight of his life at Angola.

The seminary was an example of the change in Angola's culture, creating a climate of safety and community, transforming lives (like Jesse Deters's), and impressing such varied celebrities as Barbara Walters and Joyce Meyer. Walters came to Angola at the time of the Indiana execution of Timothy McVeigh for ABC's *20/20*. She had forgotten her clip-on earrings, so after the warden met her at the Baton Rouge airport, a stop was made at Wal-Mart. ("Everyone in the South must have pierced ears!" Walters' assistant commented.) Cain was impressed by the media superstar's "friendly, down-to-earth" manner. "We sat in the car and she told me about meeting with Ariel Sharon and Yassir Arafat," he said. After production wrapped up, Walters visited the Angola Arts and Crafts Show and bought hand-carved wooden flowers for her colleagues on *The View*. "This doesn't seem like a prison," she commented to Cain. "There's no tension—everyone is so nice."

One Easter Sunday, Charles Colson returned to preach at Angola. Entertainers Charlie Daniels and Aaron Neville sang at the service as did Larry Howard and Ronnie Bryant, packed with more than two thousand inmates, and, says Cain, "did we ever have church in that arena!" The celebrity visitors each commented on the demeanor of the inmates—how they seemed so calm, so spiritual, so attentive. Cain could only respond by giving God the credit.

He also invites those of other religions to study at the seminary. "We want morality, which rehabilitates the criminal mind," he says. "Buddhist, Muslim—any religion that advocates moral character is our goal." At one point, the class contained eleven adherents of Islam. Once he asked a local Muslim imam (religious leader) how he felt about Muslim inmates attending a Baptist seminary. The imam responded that they "need a good education. Old Testament history is great, and as for New Testament studies, Jesus was a wonderful prophet."

"We teach the exclusivity of Christ," seminary director Robson said, "but we allow men from other religions to apply and become accepted if they are willing to meet all of the requirements."

One student of Islam calls his seminary training "enlightening and inviting. We're guests here; we do not insist that anyone accept our religion; nor does anyone in the seminary insist we accept theirs." Likewise, a Roman Catholic inmate who graduated from the seminary went on to build a strong Catholic church in the 850-prisoner Camp D at Angola.

One day in the shower Cain had a brainstorm. Why couldn't Angola seminary graduates go to other Louisiana prisons as missionaries? They could go in twos to other prisons to work for the chaplains, plant churches, organize Bible studies, and enhance the moral programs, serving for two years. He received Corrections Secretary Richard Stalder's blessing, and the program took off. Missionary inmates are trained, as any pastor would be, in counseling and can help the inmates when troubles arise—loss of a loved one, divorce, other needs. And, in helping the inmates, the prison is helped as the culture grows more positive. Cain comments, "If I were an atheist warden, I would want this environment in my prison because it helps ensure my success as a warden."

He likens the inmate minister program to any church that needs her own pastor, rather than relying on outside speakers. As the inmate minister programs grew and as the church grew, Cain and his team realized the need for prison chapels. "It is important that as the church grows, we build the temple. The prison chapel is an island of freedom, a holy place—it is not prison," he reflects.

Two days after the Easter Sunday when Chuck Colson preached at Angola, Cain was driving in a thunderstorm to Baton Rouge. His cell phone rang and he could barely hear over the storm, but he could hear enough to understand that one of Colson's supporters, Stuart Irby of Jackson, Mississippi, was asking questions about the prison chapel. "How much did it cost?" Irby asked. About $200,000, the warden told him, just for materials because inmates provide the labor. "Don't you need four more chapels?" Irby asked.

"Yes, we do—real bad," Cain told him. As the lightning flashed, Irby said, "When can you come to Jackson, Mississippi, and pick up a check? God has laid on my heart the desire to help you build another chapel."

"I can come right now," Cain responded. They laughed, and the following Tuesday he drove to Jackson to pick up the check. The Irbys had one condition, that Cain try to get the Mississippi State Penitentiary to establish the Bible college Cain promised, and classes began at Parchman in September 2004, following a meeting and support from the governor and other officials.

What of separation of church and state? The warden seems unconcerned about the criticism. He and others on his staff cite statistics that show the positive impact that moral rehabilitation has had at Angola. More important—as we shall see—are the stories of real men, trying at last to make something good out of their lives.

CHAPTER 7

THE BISHOP OF ANGOLA

They made him a guard when he went to Angola as an inmate. It sounds absurd—the notion of giving a convicted murderer the right to carry a rifle and control the actions of others incarcerated for the same kinds of crimes.

But this was more than forty-five years ago, when the Louisiana State Penitentiary was a horrible prison, a place where the inmates largely ran the show through intimidation and violence. The state spent as little money as it could to operate Angola. It was cheaper to install "trusted" inmates as guards than to hire and pay professional corrections officers.

So Eugene Tanniehill, DOC #533591, barely twenty years old, became a guard, wearing a khaki uniform and toting a gun that, fortunately, he never had to fire.

Tanniehill, now seventy-two, is one of many older inmates now serving life sentences who bridge the gap between the notorious, old Angola and the prison that today attracts national attention from criminal justice experts for its innovations. He recalls with great clarity, as though it was yesterday, the terrifying atmosphere at Angola when he arrived in the early 1960s.

"It was a place of violence. It was best to be afraid."

Fear. That was the most appropriate word to describe the overarching attitude of inmates at the prison then. You worked in fear. You ate in fear. You slept in fear. Even when you had some free time and the opportunity to play cards or shoot hoops, you never knew when something awful might happen to you.

The guards weren't the only inmates capable of spreading destruction and despair at Angola. There were predators—mean men, seemingly without souls, who had come to the prison after committing vicious crimes and saw the situation as ripe for violence and oppression. They preyed on weaker inmates, forcing sexual favors or extorting meager funds from those who happened to have accumulated them from family members who visited on occasion. Those unable to stand up to the predators, those who would not fight back, had no recourse but to succumb to the pressure. Others did resist, and many of them died, beaten or stabbed to death, sometimes in the early morning hours while they slept fitfully.

Few escaped the horrors of Angola. Even those who were not victimized directly still bore the deep, lasting scars of the emotional trauma that engulfed the men around them daily. You could not help but be traumatized seeing someone cruelly abused or even killed.

The brutality of the Angola of yesteryear left its indelible mark on Eugene Tanniehill as well. But he does not brood over what he and others endured. The impact of a sentence for murder, "life plus twenty-five years," became the backdrop for a remarkable, life-changing experience. Along the way Tanniehill has pointed countless men who now call him the "Bishop" to commit their lives to something bigger and better than themselves.

Eugene Tanniehill had no problem serving as an inmate guard, making twenty-four dollars a month, a princely sum for a prisoner, enjoying more privileges than those he supervised. "In a sense, I was a free man even in prison. I had that uniform and a gun, and people respected me, or so I thought. I think now that they just were in fear of me. I frightened them, and it didn't bother me a bit to do so."

Tanniehill served as a guard for eleven years and two months. He was twenty years old when he killed someone. Born and raised in Colfax, a sleepy little hamlet in central Louisiana, he got married and sought to start a family. But, he says, "I had no use for wisdom. I had a lack of knowledge, with no sense of direction, or vision for life. I was under the power of darkness."

One night, Tanniehill and his young wife went drinking at a local tavern. As the evening wore on, the alcohol flowed. The liquor dulled his common sense and erased the inhibitions that might have held a natural impulse in check. Someone said something, or at least Tanniehill thought he said something, that irritated his wife. The young husband grabbed her hand and hustled her out the door. But then he killed a man, something he regretted from the very moment he committed the murder.

Tanniehill does not dwell on the specifics, nor make any excuses for what he did. His victim was a Pentecostal preacher, a local pastor. Tanniehill does not say what the man was doing in that tavern, nor use it as an excuse for his own misconduct. He says directly, condemning himself with his words: "I slew a man of God. I was a heathen and I destroyed a man of God."

The judge told Tanniehill that he would spend what amounted to eternity in prison.

Think about it for a moment. It is harsh enough to dole out a sentence of life without the possibility of parole. Life means exactly that—a prisoner serving life leaves Angola in a casket, in a hearse, when he's dead. The judge sentencing Tanniehill added an exclamation point, as it were, with that additional twenty-five years. Tanniehill, you see, had been in Angola before and been assaulted. It was as though he were ensuring that, if by chance the law ever changed regarding life sentences, Tanniehill would still have to serve another twenty-five years in prison before he'd be eligible for release.

And so this young man was shipped to Angola, a place he knew, because others had told him, to be a hellhole of a prison. But it was not his worst nightmare come true. He served as a guard. He got those extra privileges that he enjoyed. He even continued to drink alcohol, homemade brew that he and other inmates concocted in the shadows of their cells. It was rotgut stuff, but it tasted good.

But things changed. As the years went by, Angola entered into an enormous transformation, a sea change brought on by federal court orders in the 1970s.

Federal Judge E. Gorden West in Baton Rouge had read prisoner petitions claiming even their most minimal civil rights were being ignored. He recoiled in disgust as he interviewed prisoners and heard their awful stories. He examined the penurious manner in which the state of Louisiana administered criminal justice and found it inexcusably lacking. He saw a penitentiary totally out of control, and he set about to change conditions.

No one dared to challenge the judge from issuing sweeping orders, even those who believed that he was dreadfully wrong for trying to improve a place meant to warehouse "vicious killers" who deserved whatever ill treatment they got. Those satisfied with Angola's semi-medieval, dog-eat-dog conditions complained bitterly about the unfettered power of a federal judge whose lifetime congressional appointment and authority made him the equivalent of a king within his courtroom domain.

The prisoners who understood the potential impact of the judge's edicts cheered. And they kept filing petitions whenever the state of Louisiana dragged its feet and improvements at Angola seemed to stall.

Some changes would become immediately apparent. No longer would inmates serve as guards, carrying weapons and watching over other prisoners. Gradually, too, physical conditions would improve. Money would be spent on equipment and programming. The state's secretary of corrections and the prison's administrative staff would answer to the judge. In essence, he would become Angola's de facto warden and would oversee conditions, however long it took to make the place better for inmates

whose punishment was supposed to be serving long sentences, not enduring predators and frightful living conditions.

Eugene Tanniehill, too, experienced a sea change in 1963, a transformation that would have protected and nurtured him even if no federal
judge eventually intervened at Angola. Tears well in his eyes as he recalls
the event that changed his life.

He was serving as a guard in a watchtower, making sure no one tried
to escape. It happened from time to time. Yet on this night he remained
totally oblivious, as usual, to the mayhem playing out, as usual, within the
prison camp directly beneath him.

Tanniehill detested what he had become. It wasn't enough to know
that no one would mess with him, that he had this special status and the
privileges accompanying it. He needed something far more important that
life had never given him—a peace and composure that could supplant his
insatiable reliance on booze.

For too long, alcohol had maintained total control over Eugene
Tanniehill. It was an insidious influence, self-imposed and self-abused,
nothing that anyone, not even a powerful federal judge, could order away.
Though he might enjoy the stature of serving as a guard high in a tower,
he was still a prisoner, locked up in a dungeon of his own making. He
knew that when he was drunk he could do awful things.

"It was a tool that the enemy had," Tanniehill recalled, referring to
his inability to turn away from what many euphemistically call "demon
rum." He knew that without help from somewhere, from someone greater
than himself, he could not control his abuse of alcohol. It tantalized and it
enslaved him.

So on this night in November, Eugene Tanniehill cried out in the
darkness, not knowing if anyone would answer. "I wanted to give up
alcohol. I wanted to turn away from what I had done with my life."

Someone heard him. God answered, Tanniehill said.

"I don't think a person can ever forget the transforming power of
God's grace. Sometimes it takes deep tragedy before someone will repent.
For me it was what I had done, and what I was likely to do, because of my

love of alcohol. I could see that night how God in His goodness and His grace had led me to repentance."

As he spoke, Tanniehill pointed to his chest and said, "He came into this building, and I became a changed man." The inmate did not totally understand what had happened. Yet he knew he had experienced something truly miraculous.

"I could not explain that in a lifetime—how could I explain a mystery? I just know I ended up being a changed man that night. I knew my sin had been forgiven—that I did not have to rely on alcohol any longer."

Eugene Tanniehill wasted no time telling others around him. "I had to tell everybody," he said with a smile. "They thought I had lost my mind."

Predictably, the skeptics jeered the story of the "new man." He endured the taunts and wisecracks of others who sought to undermine his newfound religious "high," to find out if he was for real or would lash out in response to hostility rather than turn the other cheek. But Tanniehill found solace in his Bible and in prayer, and he soon realized that the men around him "were blind to the reality of the existence of Jesus Christ." He also became convinced that "to live a godly life means suffering persecution. All hell is coming at you, trying to make you renounce your faith— but God worked through me to get to other prisoners."

Slowly, as those around him realized how different Tanniehill had become, they stopped the harassment and began to draw closer and ask questions of this man who would not return insult for insult, fight back, or any longer share a cup of homemade brew.

"Let men see your good works," he said, describing the change in attitudes that occurred over time. "When they found out that I was realistic through all of the trials and tribulations, they started to repent. One of the greatest movements is when men can see a difference between the world and you."

But, this being prison, the taunts didn't completely go away. Tanniehill remembers the harsh, cutting words: "What are you thanking God for, nigger?"

"When I was despised—cussed out—I would extend love to them," he says now. "When men would throw human waste at me, I would try to minister to them."

And now he is the Bishop of Angola, and the spiritual leader of the Angola Nondenominational Church. It is an unofficial title, one that Eugene Tanniehill believes God conferred on him in the early 1980s. The title, in all probability, has conferred on him far greater respect and honor than he might have ever received as a free man.

Tanniehill is the principal inmate preacher at Angola, speaking not just on Sundays but throughout the week in the prison camps. He is never without a well-thought-out message. He speaks, mostly extemporaneously, content formed around solid, biblical exposition, exhortation lively and strong, just shy of fire and brimstone. His arms are raised, his long fingers pointing, punctuating the air, to emphasize key phrases as he paces back and forth in front of the men. He is attuned to the men's needs, and his sermons are designed to meet them.

On a typical night, in the area where the inmate concession area operates, upward of seventy-five men gather for worship. A few correctional officers slip into the back of the room. They observe but seem intent on remaining largely out of sight, determined not to interfere with the occasion. An inmate band warms up the audience, and they are soon clapping, shouting "amen," and singing. The Bishop sits to one side, joining in the celebration but aware that this time there will be not only an opportunity to rejoice but also to share the sorrows of a gospel band member. The man's mother has died, suddenly and unexpectedly, and he has not yet been told as the service gets underway. Outside the concession area, in a small room, the prison's Chaplain Toney, and Tanniehill inform the man of this awful loss and comfort him. They tell him he does not have to perform on this night, that he can grieve there in the room, by himself. But he chooses to go out with them, to pick up his guitar, and accompany the singers.

When the bandleader tells the men what has happened, that "A.J.," the guitarist, has suffered a grievous loss, first Tanniehill and then many others approach him as he strums his instrument to the music. They lay hands on his shoulders and whisper prayers and words of encouragement into his ear. (Later the man tells a visitor how much the expressions of sympathy meant to him on that night. "The men have become my family," he says.)

Then Tanniehill takes over. He exhorts the men to seek God, to commit their lives to Him, to realize that they can still lead victorious lives even as they serve life sentences at Angola. He moves back and forth, back and forth, his voice loud and commanding. Perspiration breaks out across his forehead. He wipes at it with a white handkerchief. He moves quickly from one spot to another, and the boundless energy he transmits to his audience makes it hard to accept the fact that the preacher is in his seventies. The men respond enthusiastically, clapping, smiling, and even laughing as Tanniehill shares an amusing sidebar to his message.

He goes on for forty minutes, and no one stirs or seems anxious to leave. Then he is done.

The Bishop often meets one-on-one with inmates seeking guidance and answers to their problems. He also travels outside the penitentiary with inmates who have formed first-rate gospel bands and singing groups. They appear in churches and religious settings to enthusiastic audiences throughout the state of Louisiana. They are "main acts" in themselves, yet also serve to warm up the audience with their music, so that Tanniehill will quickly grab their attention when he stands to preach. A visit by the Bishop and an Angola gospel band often become a highlight worship experience for ordinary church members, plainly in awe to see God's grace and power at work in a group of men who have murdered or committed other violent crimes.

The fact that groups from a maximum-security prison can tour, largely unfettered, to appeal to free people is, when you think about it awhile, quite amazing. It seems apparent that the churches where they perform do not know what to expect when they show up at the door. The men are not dressed in convict uniforms. They are not shackled. No guards, weapons drawn, stand to protect church members from the convicts.

Nothing about the inmates' outward appearances distinguishes them from the rest of the worshipers. They are wearing white T-shirts, dark-colored sweaters and jackets, and blue jeans that lap over the tops of their sneakers. A single correctional officer accompanies them, and he is unarmed. But he is prepared to respond should trouble arise.

The opportunity to travel is another testament to Warden Burl Cain's willingness to take calculated risks. He wants people to see that Angola's inmates are not a bunch of murderous predators. He wants them to realize that God is at work in men's hearts. Yet he also makes it clear, as he must, that such gospel tours will end immediately if any inmate tries to take advantage of his limited freedom.

Eugene Tanniehill realizes that his influence as the Bishop has expanded since Burl Cain became the warden.

"I have seen and served under many wardens," he said. "None could fill the shoes of Warden Cain. I believe he was predestinated to serve here, that he was 'marked for it'—and that he has opened the door to Christianity at Angola.

"This has become a new penitentiary—God is working mightily in this place, in a miraculous way. The mentality at Angola today is different. Hideous crimes, premeditated murders, and willful crimes are largely a thing of the past. Corruption and violence are being shoved out. Education and rehabilitation are coming in. God's Spirit is moving in this place."

As this book was being written, the Bishop had served forty-five years in Angola, his life sentence plus twenty-five years still in effect. Still, Tanniehill expects to get out of prison someday when, he says, God is ready to release him. He remains philosophical about if and when that time will come.

"When a judge sentences a man to a life sentence, it's life and you've got to live it. It's like getting a two-thousand-piece picture puzzle, and now you've got to put together. You've got to put your life together. Get your mind right. Recognize that God has a job for you to do, and a duty to perform . . .

"When you come up here, it's up to you—you can surrender to do right or to do wrong. My choice was that I was going to make it."

Tanniehill believes that many men at Angola want to do right, yet are held captive by the same influences that caused them to commit horrific crimes in the first place. "We've got demonic, satanic, invisible forces of darkness at Angola—beyond human nature—trying to make the men here do bad things."

Eugene Tanniehill is the kind of inmate whom Warden Cain believes has paid the price, has been rehabilitated, and should be set free. It is not his responsibility to recommend pardons, nor does he serve on the state pardon board. For that matter, Cain cannot even make a formal recommendation to the board on behalf of someone like Tanniehill, who did come up for a pardon in 1997.

"I asked for clemency, and I was granted a sixty-year pardon," the Bishop said. That meant that he could be freed once he served a term of sixty years, still a long ways off, yet far better than life plus twenty-five. Had the governor, who must approve all pardons, accepted the board's recommendation, Tanniehill conceivably could leave Angola—an old man in his eighties, yet still alive and free.

But the governor rejected the request. The pardon board's recommendation sat on his desk for seven years. He left without signing it. Some say the Bishop wept when he realized that the pardon recommendation had lapsed and he would have to apply again someday.

Yet Tanniehill denies the story.

"God doesn't use crybabies. We don't show Him tears. We show Him endurance—boldness—forbearance."

Does he expect someday to leave Angola?

"Yes, I do. If one day is as a thousand years to God, what is forty-five years? They that wait on the Lord shall renew their strength as eagles. I can wait. God is molding, shaping, re-creating me. I have a vision that I will get out. God will release me when He is ready—nothing can stop that when the time is right. In the meantime, God is using me here at Angola for the benefit of the church. I've been following a dream for forty-five years to see the welfare of the church, to lead men to God."

When Eugene Tanniehill came to Angola, he left behind a wife and a small child. Over the years, he stopped hearing from them, and he has no idea where they are now. In their place, he has become part of a former guard's family. He said he pointed the guard in the direction of Jesus, and he made a commitment to serve God.

"They adopted me, and I'm grateful to call them my family."

When he discusses the impact that the Bishop has had at Angola, Burl Cain speaks carefully, choosing his words well. "A person of his stature is in God's hands," he says. "I know Eugene wants to get out, and he ought to be free. There are other men here, men who are older and have changed their lives, who should be considered for release. Angola should be a place for predators, not dying old men who have been rehabilitated."

Then the warden pauses.

"And yet, I sometimes wonder what would happen to the Bishop on the outside. I think of the impact the Bishop is having here, of the lives he is touching, of the opportunities he has to speak on behalf of God to desperate men whose lives are in shambles. Where else but Angola could he have that kind of influence? I've said to him, 'When you leave, you'll leave a great void—you're going to get out when God wants you out, and God may never want you out.'"

The Bishop often does not describe the details of the crime that got him sent to Angola, seemingly forever ago. But when prompted, he speaks almost eloquently of the event and how it ultimately changed his life. "I had been drinking when I did that. I was just a heathen, and I destroyed a man of God—God's property—one of His people. He fell to his death calling out to the Lord . . ."

Then Eugene Tanniehill clapped his hands and smiled. "I had spirit eyes even then, before I became a Christian. I didn't know I had that. I saw the man I killed being lifted up and ascending. God showed me there is a part of man that cannot die . . . and that I would have to come to grips with that."

The Bishop said he looked down at his hands and saw the slain preacher's blood covering them. He said the stain has never been erased.

"But now it's the blood of Jesus, and He has embraced me with it."

CHAPTER 8

TROUBLESHOOTING

The two worst nightmares of a prison warden are a riot and a hostage situation. Burl Cain has never experienced the former, but in 1999 he was confronted with the latter—hostages had been taken at his prison. In his own words:

"The call came in as I was driving to Baton Rouge. The control center told me we had hostages at Camp D. I told them I would be there as soon as I could. I was about thirty-five miles from the prison. My mind was racing. I paused and said a prayer that no one would be injured, and that God would give me wisdom and strength to deal with this situation. I immediately called Secretary of Corrections Richard Stalder at home. He answered and I was relieved. I told him, 'Secretary Stalder, we have hostages at Angola. I don't know any details, but come to Angola as soon as you can.'

"My Suburban (which the state supplies) is fast, and I drove as fast as I could with blue lights flashing and sirens blaring. Just before entering the small town of St. Francisville, I drove over a hill and the road was blocked by a traffic accident. I told the state trooper I had to get through, that I had hostages at the prison. He got on the side running board of the Suburban and rode flagging me through the maze of wrecked cars and emergency vehicles. The Louisiana State Police really came through, and later that night their tactical team would respond to the prison to offer assistance.

"While en route to Angola that night, I was in constant contact with Assistant Warden Darrel Vannoy, the chief warden for security, and his Assistant Warden David Bonnette. They had assembled the tactical team, and I told them to assault the building if they felt they could rescue the hostages without injury. This was not possible because the hostages were located in a secure building with steel prison doors, and access would be extremely hard unless we could get the hostage takers to open the door.

"When I arrived at the front gate of the prison, I sped through and drove the four miles to Camp D, at the back of the prison farm, as fast as I could. Time is of the essence in a hostage situation. There is usually a short window of opportunity before the hostage takers can get organized and develop a strategy. If you can resolve it quickly, you can avoid the long siege that can go on for days in hostage situations. Such a siege is a torment we can only imagine for the hostages. My goal was to rescue them as soon as possible and without injury—preferably to anyone.

"Warden Vannoy had one of the hostage takers on the phone, and when I walked into the room, I took the phone. I could see the West Feliciana sheriff, Bill Daniel, and his chief deputy, Ivy Cutrer—also Warden Sheryl Ranatza, the deputy warden, and Assistant Warden Paul Perkins. All were looking at me, and there was only silence. I said into the phone, 'Hello, who is this?'

"The prisoner said, 'We want to talk to the U.S. Justice Department, the FBI, and the U.S. Attorney.' That made me mad, and I told him to let my people go and do it now, or else. I felt like Moses must have felt, because I felt desperation—wanting him to just let them go. The more I talked, the madder I got, and told him to let me talk to one of the hostages. He did—she was a female correctional officer. She told me she was OK,

1. Khaki back guard (inmate) supervising "Big Stripes." (Circa 1950s)

2. Big Stripes at chow. (Circa 1950s)

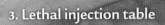

3. Lethal injection table

4. Point Lookout Cemetery

5. Warden Burl Cain

6. Cellblock keys

7. Dormitory

8. Cell

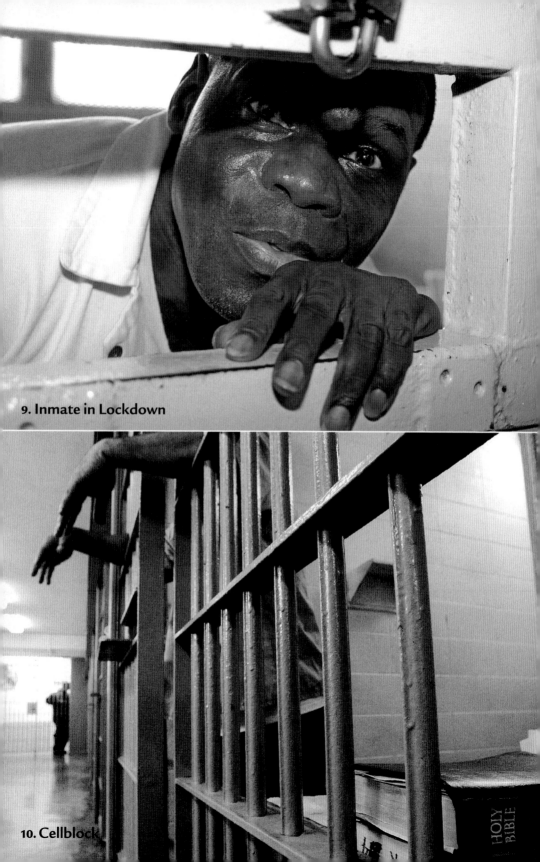

9. Inmate in Lockdown

10. Cellblock

11. Front Gate

12. Gun Guard

13. Lake Killarney, an "oxbow lake" of the Mississippi River on Angola's land

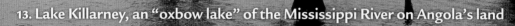

14. Sally Port

15. Field Line

16. Inmate Hobby Craft rocking chair

17. Inmate Hobby Crafters

18. Inmate Hobby Crafters — Wood Workers

19. Prayer Circle at Rodeo

20. Glory Riders

21. Wild Cow Milking Buckle

22. Warden Cain with media at Rodeo

23. Bronc Riding

24. Rough Rider — Johnny Brooks

25. Randy "Country" Ellis with Warden Cain

26. Brian Dietrich at the Angola Rodeo Crafts Show

27. Ron Hicks teaches at the Baptist Seminary

28. Kerry Myers (right) interviews an inmate craftsman for *The Angolite*

29. Ashanti Witherspoon

30. Gary Shaw

31. A. J. Freeman

32. Billy Fallon

33. "Bishop" Eugene Tanniehill

34. Ron Hicks

35. Lane Nelson

36. Warden Burl Cain

37. Prayer

38. Worship

and I promised her I would come get her. 'Just hang on and do what they say,' I told her.

"The hostage taker and I began talking again, and I told him to let the hostages go, and do it now. I told him, 'I am your mama and your daddy, and you're talking to no one but me, and I plan for this to be over before anyone gets here to question my authority.'

"There were six hostage takers, and I knew all of them did not want to die. Surely one or two would give up. The secure door would have to open to let them out; when it did, it would never close again until the hostages were rescued.

"I just had to get the door open. I knew that if we blew the door with explosives, the hostages could be harmed before they could be rescued. I had to scare, threaten, intimidate some of them so they would give up.

"Finally after a few minutes, some of the hostage takers realized they'd better get out of there, because I had convinced them that we—the tactical team—were coming, and that would be bad for them. I told them I would let them go if they let my people go. We would just all stand down—them and us. Just let the hostages go and it would be over; no one would be hurt. I told them they know I keep my word, and it works both ways. If I tell you we are coming to take you out and rescue the hostages, we will, and if I tell you we will all stand down if you release them, we will.

"Three hostage takers said they wanted out—would I send a note of amnesty? That was the break I was waiting for. My threats had paid off. I told them I would bring such a note. I quickly wrote it and read it to them. They said, 'OK, now come alone.' I flared again and said, 'Don't tell me what to do. *I* am running this; *I* am in control. I'll bring who I want.'

"I started out the door to deliver the note and told Warden Perkins to put a pistol in his belt. 'And do *not* let me be taken hostage,' I said. 'Shoot me or them, but don't let me be taken hostage.' We were going to rescue hostages, not give them more. I asked Warden Vannoy, 'Is the sniper in place?' He responded yes. I told him, 'Be ready.'

"The hostage taker could see me as I pounded on the small secure window in the door. They had the door barricaded with locker boxes.

These were moved over and the door unlocked. As soon as I heard the lock release, I jerked the door open and a long arm reached beside my leg and grabbed the keys out of the lock. That arm belonged to Secretary of Corrections Richard Stalder, and with him was Dixon Correctional Institute Warden Jimmy LeBlanc. Boy, was I glad to see them.

"Immediately the inmates saw the sniper, and I told him to get out of sight. One inmate ran out as soon as the door opened and ran over to Assistant Warden Vannoy. He told him Captain David Knapps was hurt real bad. Two others asked to sign the note and actually wanted it. I gave it to them after we all signed it, me included, and out they came. One of the other hostage takers asked me not to bury him at Angola. I told him, 'No one needs to die tonight. Just give me the hostages.' He said, 'No, now get out and let me lock the door.' I told him it was 'my door, and I'm coming in.'

"I did not have a clue as to what weapons they had. It didn't matter; we were coming in. The hostages had to be rescued. I pushed over the barricade and in I went. Secretary Stalder was right behind. I went to the first door, where the female hostage was located, as well as two hostage takers. Secretary Stalder went to the next door. There were several inmates inside that room. Warden Perkins covered the room with the pistol, and Secretary Stalder rescued the lieutenant who was one of the hostages. He was hiding under blankets. He had been beaten but could walk.

"I could see the female hostage on the floor. I would push the door open; the two hostage takers would close it. One had a homemade knife. He said he would kill her if I came in. I told him no one had to die, just give up. Finally, after a minute or so of opening and closing the door, he said, 'You haven't looked in the bathroom yet.' Secretary Stalder went there, and he looked at me down the hall with a strange expression. He said, 'Captain Knapps is dead.' We knew it was time to end it.

"Our eyes connected; the decision was made. 'Go' was the word for the shooters behind me to do their job. I stepped aside as Secretary Stalder and I said 'Go.' Both hostage takers were hit; one died as he lunged for the hostage. She was behind the door by now. The bullet hit the wall, ricocheted, and hit her assailant between the eyes. He died on the spot. The other, though critically wounded with a head shot, survived to stand trial with four others for the murder of Captain Knapps. He had fought them for the keys and lost his life—a true hero.

"Captain Knapps was rushed to the prison medical facility. At the front of Camp D, we all got on our knees. Every officer and employee and I prayed that somehow God would please spare him. We knew he was probably dead, but one of the EMTs said maybe he had detected a heartbeat. We had to pray."

David Knapps, a sixteen-year veteran of the prison staff, became only the fourth officer in the history of Angola to lose his life in the line of duty.

The hostage episode, coupled with an aborted escape attempt one month earlier by a handful of inmates on Death Row, might have been sufficient to cost Burl Cain his job. Yet his record and the success he was having in changing the prison's culture allowed him to survive, and he concluded that neither incident would force him to change his philosophy about running Angola.

Cain knew, even before Captain Knapps's death, that tragic events are going to occur on occasion in a maximum-security prison. When they do, the warden must respond without hesitation and show that he means business. The warden knew he could not allow inmates bent on escaping, taking hostages, or refusing to abide by prison rules to gain the upper hand.

Of course, no warden is a one-man show. Angola's correctional officers undergo annual training to improve their professionalism. At one time in the not-too-distant past, the prison's security staff operated with virtual impunity, abusing inmates and gaining "respect" by force and intimidation. Today, the officers attend courses to help them achieve a high standard of conduct. Training begins when men and women are hired to work at Angola.

The programs are held on prison grounds in what is now called the David C. Knapps Correctional Officer Training Academy.

To build a positive prison culture where men can be transformed and live as productive "neighbors," certain things have to happen—and certain things have to *not* happen. Order must be maintained; troublemakers must be isolated. Troublemakers, Cain knows, derail progress. Two such prisoners have been in extended lockdown in single cells for many years after they killed a security officer. Cain has ignored the vocal protests of a group that has been championing an effort to return the two men to the general prison population. He and his staff believe they will only stir up more trouble if they can live in the dormitory-style settings that many of Angola's inmates enjoy—because they have earned the right to enjoy it.

Cain recognizes that all men at Angola desperately desire to win their freedom someday. A few will do anything to get out, and they are the most dangerous. These are inmates who riot or try to escape or take correctional officers as hostages or even attempt suicide. Such incidents, while admittedly rare, become a warden's worst nightmare because they draw negative public attention to the prison. Maintaining vigilance against such acts, all the while striving to change a prison's environment for the better, can create tremendous stress on a warden. The "reformers" often fail because they cannot reconcile the threat with the opportunity. Too often, the progressive efforts succumb when something terrible occurs in their prisons. The public outcry forces the "reformers" to revert to warehousing.

It is to Burl Cain's credit that he remains doggedly determined not to fold under pressure—and that he prefers prevention over putting out fires. "Violence is like fire," he says. "It is better to prevent fire than to fight fire. If you have to fight fire, you might get burned."

Another sort of pressure can come from crime victims' families. Cain feels deep compassion for the families of crime victims. He also recognizes their influence with parole and pardon boards. He knows that a prisoner's eventual freedom is likely to depend in large part on the man's willingness to reconcile with the family of his victim. That often in itself dooms any inmate's hope of eventual freedom. Those who have lost loved ones to violent criminal acts often refuse to consider that the perpetrator has paid enough of a price.

On occasion, though, family members may be willing to meet with the man who killed a relative. They may want to know how a loved one died, and whether he or she suffered in the end. They are hoping to gain some closure on an act that has haunted them for years. They may be willing to sit across from the perpetrator and look into his eyes—and, by extension, into his very soul—to see if he is truly the monster they have made him out to be. The inmate, for his part, has the opportunity to express his deepest regret for what he has done and, perhaps, even to obtain a measure of forgiveness.

Cain and his staff have initiated a handful of carefully scripted sessions where the victim's family met the perpetrator. The warden explains: "It gives the family a chance to ask questions, to find out if their loved one felt any pain, if he or she said anything before dying . . . what was said. It may become an opportunity for family members to begin to heal. And they may discover that the man who did this awful thing to the victim isn't that monster they created in their minds. Finally, if he means it, the inmate can show genuine remorse. He can say, with conviction, 'I'm so sorry.'"

The sessions are not designed to produce get-out-of-jail free cards for inmates. But they do begin to break through the atmosphere of fear that surrounds most people, beginning with the victims' families, when they consider that someone who has killed or maimed may be released from prison. "No one is going free from Angola until the victims' families aren't afraid of them anymore," Cain declares. "The families have suffered, been tormented by their loss, and shouldn't have to be afraid in the dark because the man who did something awful to their loved one is now on the outside and might come after them as well. It's important that families of victims can live without fear.

"Initiating inmate-victim reconciliation is not easy. Yet even when there is risk that a session might blow up, you have to say yes, let's do it. When it works, there is healing on both sides. The victim's family forgives, and the inmate can cleanse his past."

The key, of course, is whether a family believes the perpetrator is truly remorseful or is simply playacting, with only the goal in mind of somehow getting out of Angola.

Reconciliation in itself is not the door to freedom, since inmates first must win the right to make their case before the pardon board. But it is essential. No matter what kind of progress an inmate has made in prison, or the accomplishments he has achieved, or the length of his incarceration, the board likely will dismiss a petition out of hand if the victim's family or local law enforcement objects. Victims' advocacy groups also can derail a prisoner's efforts to win a pardon. Representatives of those groups appear without fail at the pardon board hearings. A prisoner who has support from the victim's family may still get an unfavorable response if the victims' advocacy spokesman opposes release. And life at Angola stretches on.

Trouble also happens when privileges are abused. When the warden first came to Angola, Class A trustees with excellent disciplinary records enjoyed the privilege of visiting family in a beautiful park nestled along the road on one side of the prison. Small, grassy hills were shaded by large oak trees; loved ones could visit in privacy on park benches under gazebo-like shelters. A concession stand sold food for grilling and picnicking, adding to the atmosphere of an enjoyable family outing.

But one thing was prohibited.

Not long after Cain assumed his post, his good friend and cousin, Louisiana state legislator Herman Ray Hill, called to tell the warden a young woman from his district was pregnant by an Angola inmate—one with park visiting privileges. Cain took immediate action, terminating the inmate's park visits and ordering removal of the waist-high walls around the gazebos. Still, sexual encounters continued at the park, until finally the warden called a meeting in the all-purpose arena where both the rodeo and religious gatherings are held.

As the eight hundred inmates gathered in the arena, most of them thought Cain was going to call a halt to park visits, as he had done in the past. The warden, however, had different ideas. He said, "I'm not closing the park this time," elaborating on the benefits of the park to the community. But, he continued, it's irresponsible to father a child and not be able to provide for that child, to hold it, to care for it. Think of the hardship on the mother, caring for a child alone. The road to moral rehabilitation, he declared, was not one of reckless irresponsibility. "I won't be part of that." How, he challenged his men, could one be so irresponsible?

"I don't want the park. It's your park. Take care of it, be responsible for it. But if you don't want the park, just keep on abusing it."

Two weeks later, an inmate and his visitor had sex in the park—and, as Cain said later, "They gave the park back to me." Cain and his team were sad but not surprised; after all, moral change at Angola was in its infancy at the time. Today, perhaps, the outcome might be different. But problems keep coming up, as in any prison. And Cain keeps telling the inmates—this is how it is.

Recently Cain was escorting a group of visitors through Angola's main prison, which houses about twenty-four hundred inmates in dormitories and cell blocks. A group of inmates, members of a Dale Carnegie chapter, congregated around folding tables in a long recreation room eating dinner and watching a video movie on a large screen. At one end behind a counter sat a female guard, again unarmed and largely ignored by the inmates as they enjoyed the film, a comedy starring Adam Sandler. As the visitors entered, the inmate who is president of the Dale Carnegie chapter stepped in front of the screen and motioned to temporarily stop the video. Then he greeted Burl Cain. The warden asked to address the group for a few minutes, a request instantly granted.

The inmates became quiet and attentive as Cain conversed with them in a soft Southern drawl. There is no bark in the voice of this short, stout, energetic man in his early sixties. Yet the inmates know he can bite, and bite hard, if necessary. The stress of the responsibilities of managing Angola is not readily apparent on the face of the warden. He moves easily, without fear or apprehension, throughout the prison main camp, his guests in tow without any guards to shield them from the inmates.

Indeed, Cain, both affable and confident, seems to enjoy these informal contacts with the inmates, because it allows him to be both accessible and, in a very real sense, vulnerable to them in situations like this. Yet, at the same time, it becomes immediately clear to the guests that there is an invisible shield separating the warden from the inmates, even when they whisper to him respectful pleas requesting that he right some perceived wrong they believe they have experienced. Cain calls this separation from the inmates his "threshold." It is a barrier over which no prisoner can be allowed to cross. Even when he smiles over something the inmate next to him might have said, the warden still makes clear by the tone in his voice that he is not a friend or colleague but the taskmaster of a huge prison where the man is incarcerated, his freedom gone, likely forever.

Now, as Cain took the floor, the inmates clapped approvingly, as if acknowledging an old friend—even though they knew he was bringing bad news. Most of the men had already heard about the ugly incident that occurred the week before. They had a pretty good idea what the warden intended to do about it. They knew Cain and his staff could not ignore the outrage committed by an inmate whose actions were now likely to cost them a precious privilege—in this case, their microwave ovens.

Anywhere from sixty-four to seventy-five men live in Angola's dormitories. These inmates have learned to live together in an awkward community, in large open rooms on cots, with easy access to enjoy each other's company or, if they prefer, to bury their noses inside paperback books.

These inmates enjoy a certain measure of institutional freedom. Specifically, in this instance, it is the use of microwave ovens to heat popcorn snacks and water. Others, held inside single or double cells elsewhere on the prison grounds, have yet to achieve any privileges because, when given the opportunity in the past, they have brutalized each other or threatened the guards.

The men know well Warden Cain's philosophy: "We don't take things away from you. You give them to us" like the park. The meaning is clear. The men inside Angola have the opportunity to achieve a certain level of freedom. If they misuse or abuse it, it is rescinded.

In one dorm, two men had been grating on each other's nerves for some time, and eventually things spiraled out of control. One of them managed to smuggle a bit of honey or maple syrup or maybe a little sugar in the pocket of his blue jeans before leaving the inmate mess hall. Instead of sweetening a cup of coffee or tea, he attempted to get even with the annoying dorm mate. One evening, he sauntered over to the microwave oven, stirred whatever it was that he had smuggled for the purpose into his cup of water, then heated the mixture to a boil. Then he casually made his way toward his foe. Without warning, he threw the deadly goo at his victim, scalding his chest and arms. The stuff stuck fast to the man's skin, like hot tar on a pavement, sending him to the infirmary with second-degree burns.

Now as Warden Cain stood before this group of inmates, he hadn't quite made up his mind, but he made it clear he was leaning heavily toward removing all of the microwaves from the dorm areas. The men would have to find another way to pop corn or heat water for instant coffee, cocoa, or tea. As he explained the probable consequences of the scalding incident, the men sat listening intently. Then a few hands popped up as Cain asked if there are questions.

"Is there a chance you won't pull the microwaves?" one inmate asked.

"Not likely," the warden replied. "We can't afford another scalding. You know we don't want to have to do this, but one of you has given us no choice."

The men seemed to accept the explanation even as they held out slim hope that Cain would consider something else to make his point.

"No chance you'll give us another chance?" another inmate asked.

"Not likely."

"What about something in place of the microwaves?" another asked.

"Like what?" Cain responded.

"How about toaster ovens or small coffeepots?"

The warden nodded thoughtfully. "We'll think about it."

The men seemed pleased he was willing to consider an alternative. They knew, based on other incidents where privileges were revoked because of an inmate's misconduct, it was unlikely the microwave ovens would remain in the dormitories. At best, if they properly used whatever substitute cooking devices the prison staff provided, someday the microwaves might return. But it seemed obvious that "someday" in this case could be years down the road.

Both men involved in the scalding incident are suffering punishment as well. Already the assailant is housed in a single cell. He will not get out anytime soon. The victim, who some say was a party to provoking the fierce anger that resulted in his horrible burns, may pay a consequence as well. When he has recovered enough to be released from the prison infirmary, he could lose as-yet unspecified privileges.

When things go wrong in a maximum-security prison, someone always pays a price. Sometimes only the perpetrators suffer. The scope of lost privileges, of punishment, often depends on whether what has occurred was a surprise, or whether the prison staff was tipped off and could take measures to thwart a potentially ugly and dangerous incident. In this case, it was probable that others in the dorm knew animosity was mounting between the two inmates, and a few may even have known what one of them intended to do about it. But nobody spoke up; nobody assumed the role of "good citizen." So Cain acted.

In a maximum-security prison, there is always a danger that simmering crises will explode. Angola has seen its share of the latter. In the early 1980s, a couple of inmates took then-Warden Ross Maggio and his mother hostage and tried to use them as human shields in order to escape. The men forced Maggio to drive them through the front gate, insisting they would stab his mother if he didn't succeed in escorting them past the guards and on to freedom.

The warden, furious that he was in this predicament, was not a willing hostage. He refused to be intimidated. As he drove his captors and mother through the gate, he crashed his car into a retaining wall. In the ensuing chaos, the warden fled the vehicle and reached over and grabbed a stunned security officer's pistol. Then he raced back to the auto, where his injured mother was still in the grasp of the hostage takers. Emptying the pistol into the inmates, he killed one and wounded the other.

Cain does not explain what he would have done had he been the warden taken hostage years ago. He prefers not to engage in such speculation, to play the "what-if" game; that is counterproductive. Telegraphing what he might do when the "if" occurs tips his hand to any inmate contemplating carrying out a violent incident. Cain also knows that if he rattles a saber, and threatens to retaliate harshly in every conceivable crisis, he possibly could wreck what otherwise might have been a less-devastating, but more effective, response.

It is enough to say that Cain will act without hesitation and without agonizing later that what he did was the appropriate course. Each crisis he endures and solves provides him with greater assurance that he successfully can face down the next incident so that it does not wreck his program for Angola. The warden's staff knows he never seems mystified, incapacitated, hesitant, or reluctant in a crisis—all marks of indecisiveness that lead to a catastrophe. They know he will never give the inmates creating chaos an opportunity to gain the upper hand. And when the situation has been resolved, they know he will return to his agenda for the prison and not allow what happened to derail it.

Burl Cain also came to realize early in his stint at Angola that whenever his staff failed to act decisively and appropriately, he would have to use the incident to show them what he expected the next time. He would demonstrate dramatically—perhaps even overreacting, as it were—so no one would be forced to guess what he was supposed to do the next time he faced a crisis.

The fight between the two inmates one hot afternoon on a field at The Farm began suddenly and without warning, as these things often do. The men were part of a group of prisoners working in the field, out in one of Angola's many farm areas, cultivating a healthy, growing food crop. It is hard work, eight hours' worth, in conditions that sometimes serve to aggravate tensions that could be expected to remain in check. However, when an outburst occurs among the fieldworkers, there often is little warning.

The security officers guarding inmates on farm details know the drill. They are expected, without hesitation, to break up fights like the one that was unfolding now. It is too easy for other inmates to jump in, to escalate a two-man altercation into a full-scale riot. When a fight breaks out the security officers on duty are expected to restore order immediately, even if it means having to hurt those creating the ruckus.

On this particular afternoon, the usual complement of security officers in the field watched over a group of men. Two security officers were on horseback and carrying carbines. Their roles are the only ones requiring firearms. Each was posted some distance at each end of the inmate farm crew. The officers on horseback are positioned intentionally, at diagonal ends of the workers, so they can easily see when someone seems to be slacking off or straying from the pack—signaling, perhaps, an intent to make a run for it.

A third officer, called a "pusher," was on foot, also as usual, working alongside the men inside the invisible rectangle. He is charged with making sure none of the inmates might begin to meander or waste time. The two officers on horseback "watch his back," ensuring that he is safe within the worker crew, who are using shovels and, perhaps, sling blades, as they work within the crops. They have specific instructions they must follow whenever an incident breaks out, as it was on this day.

Perhaps the scorching sun, coupled with the fatigue of the labor, sparked the confrontation. Perhaps the two inmates had been having words all along and, well, had simply had enough of each other. In a moment, they had tossed aside their shovels and were exchanging punches. Then the fight escalated as they wrestled on the ground, swinging wildly, gouging, grappling to gain a temporary advantage in the struggle, legs splayed, tangled at first, then freed so each could launch kicks at the opponent's vulnerable limbs.

Other inmates stopped, fascinated, watching the unfolding spectacle, and murmuring, even shouting, words of encouragement to the fighters.

In a moment the "pusher" was there as well, first ordering the men to separate, then joining the fray to pull them apart. The officer soon became caught up in the frenzy and was down as well, neutralized, not only unable to stop the fight but risking serious injury as the inmates rolled in the dirt, punching and kicking each other.

In another moment, one officer on horseback galloped to the fight scene. He dismounted—intent on ending the brawl and rescuing his colleague. But he quickly became as incapacitated as well. Harvey Slater, a 20-year veteran of corrections, was hit in the back with a sling blade as he tried to stop one inmate from hitting another inmate in a field line.

The third officer on horseback, a rookie at Angola, seemed mesmerized by the chaos playing out before him. Finally he radioed for help. Still he remained atop his horse, some distance from the fight. He continued to cradle his rifle and steered his mount closer, shouting for other inmates not to move, to remain in place "or else." All obeyed. But still the scuffle went on.

In what seemed to be only a few more seconds, unarmed reinforcements—a handful of correctional supervisors working elsewhere on the grounds—responded to the radio SOS. They plowed into the crowd of fighters and onlookers, soon putting an end to the fight and rescuing their fallen comrades. Using fists, wooden black batons, and well-aimed kicks, they forced the two inmates apart. The two officers caught up in the fight took deep, frantic gulps of air as they struggled to regain their composure. They would say later on that it was a harrowing experience, one they hoped never again to repeat.

Word travels fast across a prison when something untoward occurs. News of the fight in the field soon reached the warden. Even as his security staff was restoring order and preparing to remove the two inmates who had caused the disturbance, Burl Cain arrived. He leaped from his vehicle and trotted across the field toward the group. After ascertaining that everything was under control, and hearing that the third officer had done nothing to stop the fight, Cain made his way to the young employee, who by now had dismounted.

The officer's flushed face and sagging shoulders served to indicate how rattled he was by what had happened and his failure to help end the fight. He seemed clearly chagrined and embarrassed. By now he knew how easily the brawl could have ended in tragedy had any other inmates joined the brawl and attacked the two fallen officers.

Cain wasted little time dealing with the officer.

"I grabbed his rifle from his hands," he said. "I shouted at him, 'Is there something wrong with your gun? Is that why you didn't fire it?' Then I fired the weapon into the ground. The sound of the weapon going off was deafening. 'So there was nothing wrong with your gun,' I roared. 'You just didn't use it like you've been trained to do. You failed your fellow officers when they needed you. They could have been hurt or even killed. What you did was inexcusable.'"

By now Cain was inches away from the errant officer, the warden's face becoming flushed in anger as he yelled at the man, who could only back away awkwardly as he tried in vain to deflect the withering verbal attack. The warden kept coming at him. In a moment he stunned the young officer: "You're fired. I'm taking away your gun. I want you off the prison grounds right now. I don't want to see your face again."

The crestfallen officer did not know what to do at first. Then he dropped the reins to his horse and began walking in the direction of the Angola visitors' gate. He would have walked all the way out, a mile or more, had not another sympathetic security officer offered a ride to his vehicle.

Someone hearing the fight story, and its aftermath, might assume that the warden lost his cool and overreacted. No one had been hurt, after all. Order had been restored quickly. The two inmate perpetrators were on their way to administrative detention, in solitary cells. They would have plenty of time to contemplate the foolishness of what they had done in the farm field.

But then the point of what the warden was doing is missed. The errant security officer had, in effect, exercised discretion—by not reacting appropriately—in a situation that did not *allow* for any discretion. Security officers are trained to respond to outbreaks in the field, or an attempted escape, without pausing to think about what they should do. They are supposed to act decisively, without deviation from established policies and procedures. Using discretion, failing to respond according to the book, creates the potential for disaster.

"In the field, when an inmate takes off running or begins to fight someone, we're supposed to fire a warning shot into the air," an officer explained. "If that isn't sufficient to restore order, we're to shoot a second time. We're to fire a disabling shot, to bring down whoever is creating a disturbance or trying to escape. There is no excuse for responding any other way."

What if the disabling shot kills the offender?

"We're supposed to be able to bring him down without killing him, but if that happens, we're still justified."

Warden Cain intended his outburst at the rookie security officer to send a message.

"The last thing you want to have happen in a situation like the fight in the field is for an armed officer to use discretion—in other words, to disobey. If the inmates think an officer who is armed will hesitate, that he won't shoot when he's supposed to shoot, they'll begin taking advantage of the situation. That becomes a big challenge to the safety of my staff. We can't allow that to happen.

"That's why I took the officer's rifle and fired it. I wanted the inmates to know we mean business, that if I had been there in that officer's place, I'd have restored order even if I had to shoot someone to do it."

Burl Cain loves his job, even though it is a backbreaker. He expects to stay another ten years, assuming his health holds up and he does not become that "sacrificial lamb" when a violent incident places him and the prison in jeopardy. He is active, always on the move, perhaps believing that a moving target is harder to hit. He insists he will never simply tread water, taking it easy, in his remaining time at Angola. He is open and eager to continue improving the prison environment, urging the inmates to see what they accomplish even as lifetime prisoners. Yet he remains mindful of what the people of Louisiana—his ultimate "employers"—expect. He knows they will not tolerate a vacillating warden who seems to have lost control at Angola.

Meanwhile Cain and his team keep dealing with challenges as they arise—and Angola keeps moving toward a more positive environment.

CHAPTER 9

A SHARP SLIVER OF METAL

The inmate, a trustee, knew he was in trouble. He just didn't know how much. He had always had a clean record—not perfect but clean. He had been at Angola for seventeen years, sentenced to life for a murder he committed, violently and without thinking, as an eighteen-year-old hothead. It had taken him years to get used to prison life, and years to become a trustee, but now he almost felt as though he belonged, as though this was his home, somewhere he could live out his life without fear and with some feeling of contributing.

He knew the rules, and Angola had its share. You got written up for infractions, sometimes seemingly minor, picky stuff, the kind of stuff that people on the outside would never consider worth calling you on the carpet over, let alone getting you in trouble. But this is a maximum-security prison, and the men who reside here are considered bad dudes. An inmate can get dinged for failing to keep his personal stuff in order, for sassing a correction officer, for "mixing it up" with another inmate who is always in his face.

Some inmates like to irritate the trustees, because trustees get special privileges. So they work on a trustee, intent on getting a rise out of him, knowing that if he reacts, shoves them away or takes a swing at them, he will get punished for it.

A trustee learns, if he wants to hold on to his position, to brush off the troublemakers, to take a deep breath and count to ten, and maybe ten again.

An inmate also can get written up for having contraband, maybe a jug of homebrew or a little "weed." It is a big risk to hide contraband, knowing that in all probability a corrections team—a shakedown crew—will find it during a surprise inspection of a dormitory or cell. An inmate is a fool to think he can stash something in a special hiding place where the officers won't find it.

The trustee's problem wasn't hiding something. It was losing something—something very small. He had no idea where it might be, and his boss, a correctional sergeant, a nice guy who treated him with respect, wasn't going to be happy when he learned about the loss.

The trustee worked on a small crew that mixed animal feed. He'd had the job for several years. He had mastered it to the point that the time went by too quickly. He enjoyed the hours he spent away from his dormitory working on packing oats and fodder in large burlap sacks for the prison's horses. It was a decent job, a chore that kept him outdoors, breathing fresh country air, enjoying the opportunity, on breaks, to take in the panoramic view of wide expanses, the river, and the hills. Maybe even he daydreamed sometimes, for the moment at least, that he wouldn't always be at Angola, that he wouldn't always be a lifer without possibility of parole.

Armed correctional officers mounted on horses patrol teams of inmates working on The Farm. Except for these officers and the guards monitoring the prison's entrance gate, no other staff person carries a weapon that might be taken away from him in an inmate insurrection.

Instead most correctional officers carry two-way radios to keep in constant contact with supervisors who know what to do, and quickly, in a crisis. The system of surveillance in the field, using mounted officers, is far more economical than putting a bunch of them on foot on the ground circulating around, perhaps, fifty or more inmates in a work crew. As we've seen, two mounted officers, carrying rifles, easily could see across the pack of inmates, could spot anyone thinking about wandering off, and could shout a warning when someone seems to be slacking off or drifting away. Astride a horse, an officer can fire a warning shot into the ground, if necessary, and even shoot to disable any inmate foolish enough to try to run away.

The trustee's job was to fill sacks with feed and then, using a large, gray metal, six-inch needle, sew the tops shut with thick twine. Thus secured, the feed sacks can be stacked and transported without breaking open.

The needles are considered Class A tools and, as such, must be strictly accounted for. Other Class A tools include the shovels and sling blades that inmates use for cultivation and weeding, silverware, kitchen knives, water hoses, and even electrical cords (that someone could employ to bind a guard, wrap around someone's neck, or attempt suicide). Class A tools are counted; when one is missing, it is a big deal.

The trustee had put his needle aside, carelessly, in the last few minutes, and now he could not locate it. For a moment, he didn't make the connection between the missing needle and what it might mean to his status if he couldn't find it. He looked around, scanning the work area, lifting empty burlap bags, using his hand to sweep aside scraps of animal feed on the ground, certain he'd catch the shiny glint of the needle in the sunlight. But it wasn't there. He stifled a shudder that rushed down his spine. He thought about not mentioning the missing needle, of hoping, somehow, he might not have to account for it at the end of the day. But the longer he waited, the more trouble he might be in. The sergeant wasn't going to forget to account for all of the needles when the day was done. He'd be suspicious if the trustee didn't confess to the loss until confronted about a missing needle.

So the trustee did the only thing he could to minimize the situation. He caught the attention of his sergeant:

"I can't find a needle."

"What do you mean, you can't find it? Where'd it go?"

"I don't know."

In an instant, the sergeant called time-out. Soon everyone on the crew, even the correctional officer, was searching for the needle.

At first blush, one would think that a lost needle, even a big one, was no big deal, a thin sliver of metal that might likely never turn up if it went missing, especially in an area like the barn where horse feed was being bagged. That's why there's that overworked saying about how difficult it is to find a needle in a haystack. When someone who's on the outside, and not in prison, is sewing on a button, for instance, and drops the needle so that it suddenly disappears, he takes but a moment to look for it. When he can't find it, he simply reaches for another one and finishes the job. It's the same when a seamstress loses a needle. She doesn't waste time searching for it. She just grabs another one.

But in a maximum-security prison, a lost needle can be a big issue. In the hands of an inmate, a needle like the one used to secure burlap feed bags can become a weapon, maybe even a lethal weapon. An inmate can thrust it into an eye or even the chest of another, perhaps in the dead of night. If he's crafty enough, he may get away with it, and no one will ever know who committed the horrible act.

Yet needles have legitimate use, important uses, in a prison farm setting where it is cheaper to make animal feed, bag it, and store it, than it is to buy the stuff on the outside. After all, it only costs the prison a few cents per inmate per hour to process the feed. The bags, twine, and needles are dirt cheap, so it is a good deal to employ trusted inmates—trustees—to do the work.

That means they must have access to needles. Every day the sergeant in charge hands out needles at the beginning of the work shift and then collects them at the end of the day. If he hands out fifteen, he expects to get fifteen back. He counts each one as it is turned over to him, then recounts the batch before putting the needles into a drawer for safe keeping overnight. It is not good enough to get thirteen or fourteen returned. Every trustee must hand back a needle when his work is done.

The men on the sergeant's feed crew spent a day searching for the needle. They combed the area, not once but several times, on their hands and knees. Even the sergeant got down on the ground to look for it.

But they couldn't find it. As the hours passed, the trustee who lost the needle became increasingly frantic. He kept insisting he had misplaced it, that he had not secreted it in his clothing, that he had no reason to risk his status by trying to hide the needle for some other, sinister use. The sergeant didn't respond to the trustee's explanations, refusing to look the man in the eye or give any sign that he believed him.

As it became apparent the needle would not be found, the trustee became resigned to the fate he knew he had coming. He had no idea what might be the punishment for losing the needle. But he knew, barring a miracle, he would pay a price. He just hoped it would not be severe, that it would not mean being reassigned to another, less desirable job, or—unthinkable—losing his trustee status.

It had taken him years to become a trustee. If they took the title away, it might be years before he became one again. He dreaded the thought of having to start over, of having to win the respect of the correction staff that—maybe, eventually—would allow him to become a trustee once more.

"I've got to report what's happened," the sergeant said as the search ended.

"I know," the trustee answered, resignation in his voice. "I'm in a lot of trouble, right?" Yes, you are, the sergeant's nod confirmed.

What kind of trouble, the trustee could only speculate. Punishment for various forms of wrongdoing varies in a prison. Sometimes, nothing much happens. Or you can lose privileges, like the opportunity to live in a wide-open dorm rather than a cell. Or you can lose status, being reduced from a role of a trustee, or even wind up in administrative lockdown for a period of time. Administrative lockdown might mean being transferred from a wide-open dorm to a cell in the same camp where you'd remain except for time-out to perform work duties each day. Or it might mean winding up at Camp J, and sitting all day long in a cell where you have periodic reviews for weeks or months, until the correctional staff concluded you had learned your lesson and were ready to fix the bad behavior and bad attitude that got you put there in the first place.

Thinking about all this, the trustee could only imagine what might be in store for him. His stomach was in knots as he fretted about appearing before the prison's disciplinary board, two members of the staff responsible for reviewing infractions and doling out punishment. He spent days preparing his defense, rehearsing what he would tell the disciplinary committee about the needle.

It used to be, in prisons across America, that an inmate accused of disobeying the rules felt the sting of discipline in a matter of hours, without any opportunity to explain his side of the situation that had gotten him in this predicament. But then a prisoner, now euphemistically called a jailhouse lawyer, had a novel thought. He came to realize that the Constitution's guarantee of due process meant he could not be punished severely without some kind of hearing where he could defend himself. So he sued for the right to require the prison's disciplinary authority to provide a hearing where he could put on evidence and make his case. Only then could the prison discipline him.

Some might believe that in a prison setting, where inmates are being punished for committing serious, awful offenses, "due process" is an oxymoron. Yet going to prison does not mean that someone gives up all constitutional rights, rights that are meant to protect every citizen regardless of status. Due process is important because it guarantees that before anyone faces harsh punishment, he must have a day in court to defend against the accusations.

The same due process applies for free people facing penalties for criminal and civil infractions. It is a hallmark of the American system of law and order.

Prisoners also need the protection of due process because some believe that when someone goes to jail for wrongdoing, any disciplinary action that occurs during imprisonment is simply an extension of the sentence and does not require any additional protections for the inmate. Yet the reality of imprisonment in a place like Angola is that incarceration— the loss of freedom for a period of time or even forever—*is* the punishment. Warden Burl Cain and his staff believe that anything else that happens after an inmate winds up in jail, without giving him the chance to explain his side, is piling on. Prison authorities are supposed to keep the inmates locked up, not find new, creative ways to jack up the punishment.

At Angola, as part of the due process to which an inmate is entitled, he has an opportunity to make his defense before a disciplinary board made up of two prison officials. If the charge against him could result in the loss of status or pay, he may even request a counsel substitute, functioning like a paralegal, to assist him. In some cases, the counsel substitute may research the issue in the prison law library, hoping to find a case or two that could be cited in the inmate's defense. In some cases, the counsel substitute appears before the board, serving as the inmate's lawyer. A clever counsel substitute, well versed in the law, may force the board to consider issues it might otherwise have ignored.

Even so, the chance of escaping a disciplinary hearing without some punishment is slim. At most, if an inmate is persuasive, the court might mitigate what it does, perhaps reducing the amount of time he has to spend in detention in a cell or allowing him to remain as a trustee, for example, but at a reduced grade. (There are Class A, B, and C trustees. Only Class A trustees are allowed to travel within the prison grounds without being accompanied by a correctional officer.) But it's almost certain that the inmate will pay some price.

So when he went before the disciplinary board, the trustee gave it his best shot, knowing he was fighting an uphill battle. He admitted being lax for letting the needle out of his sight—"I have no excuse for not paying attention to where I laid it down." But he insisted, almost begging, that the board should believe there was nothing for him to gain by hiding the needle so he or someone else could use it in a nefarious way later on. "I've got too much at stake to do something stupid like that," he pleaded. "I'm here for life, and I've worked hard to make a place for myself at Angola. Why would I risk what I've accomplished by hiding that needle or giving it to someone else?"

The sergeant who wrote up the incident had to agree. He said later that the missing needle might have been sucked into a long tube and become lodged in the machinery used to mix and deliver horse feed to the inmates bagging it. "You can hear a sort of clinking when we start up the machine."

Yet the sergeant did not have the discretion to ignore the lost needle, since he too was held accountable for keeping track of Class A tools. Just as he had to count the needles at the end of each workday and know that none were missing, a higher-up could, and probably would, appear to count them as well. Failure to report a missing Class A tool could cost the sergeant his job. So at day's end, he reported the apparent infraction, but without enthusiasm since he believed the trustee's explanation. There was one other thing that the sergeant could not do. He could not appear at the disciplinary hearing to put in a good word for the man. Besides, he knew the inmate was likely to learn a valuable lesson out of this fiasco—to never again let his needle out of sight.

"I hoped he would not suffer any serious consequences," the officer said later. "Having to appear before the disciplinary board was punishment enough. I wanted him back on my crew."

After the hearing, the two members of the board deliberated for less than fifteen minutes. One at first suggested punishing the man by requiring him to reimburse the prison for the cost of the needle—state property. He also argued that the trustee, whose Class A status gave him considerable freedom, be demoted. But in the end, he went along with his colleague's proposal that the board should admonish the inmate for lax behavior, and do nothing more.

"There's nothing to be gained by punishing him," both agreed. "Haven't we all lost stuff like this? Besides, the report of the sergeant who knows him best seems to vouch for his honesty."

Prison administration, Cain believes, should be appropriately compassionate and fair—never oppressive. When informed that he would pay no price for losing the needle, the trustee wept.

CHAPTER 10

SHAKEDOWNS AND PRISON BREAKS

Above all, the inmates have to be kept *in*.

Burl Cain reminisces about a couple of escape attempts from his pre-Angola days:

"While warden at Dixon Correctional Institute, we had a very good bloodhound chase team. One night an inmate escaped. I lived on part of the DCI property, and the bloodhounds were chasing the escaped prisoner toward my house. Behind my house was a cemetery. The house was on the site of McManus Plantation, and the small cemetery had a nice wrought-iron fence. These small family cemeteries were customary back in pre–Civil War times. The escaped inmate went in the cemetery. Apparently when he realized he was in a cemetery, it almost scared the life out of him. I know this because one side of the fence was torn down—the side where he exited. We continued the chase, following the dogs across the pasture to the woods. At this point we were laughing, because the foot tracks we were following had become very far apart on leaving the cemetery. He was running because the cemetery had scared him. We didn't want to follow the dogs into the woods, which were very thick with briars, vines—just really bad, not to mention real snaky looking. I told the chase team, as dog handlers are called, to wait right where he went in the woods. I told them to answer if he called out to them. I assumed he knew we were close, as he would have seen our lights. The bloodhounds are trained not to bark because a fugitive would hear the dogs and just run faster.

"I went back to my house, got my Suburban, and drove back across the pasture without the lights. Pastor Ed Jelks from Norwood Baptist Church was visiting with me that night prior to the escape. I told Ed, 'Come on and ride with me. We might need some help.' The moon was bright, and I stopped beside the woods a few hundred yards past where he went into the woods. My vehicle was equipped with a siren, police lights, and a public address system. I shut off the motor, and when all was quiet—just the moon and stars, it was a bright night—I turned on the PA system and let out a bloodcurdling howl like a lonely wolf. There was silence as the howl echoed through the woods.

"I did it again, waited . . . nothing. I know the chase team thought I was nuts. Then I howled again. This time we heard him almost scream, 'Come get me! There's haints in these woods! Come get me!' The chase team leader called out, 'Over here—run over here fast!' I howled again. He screamed again, 'Come get me! These haints are chasing me! Help!' And they would shout, 'Over here! Run and we'll help you!' And run he did! I continued to howl. He thought *haints,* as he called them, meaning ghosts, were chasing him because of the cemetery experience. He ran right through the briars and bushes. He would have frightened the snakes the way he was shouting and running—all the way into the chase team's arms."

Cain recalls another "interesting" escape from his Dixon days:

"My brother, James David, who is now a state senator but was state representative at the time, asked me to have one of his constituents' sons transferred to DCI. I accommodated my brother, requesting the transfer from the Department of Corrections. Inmate Fontenot was transferred to

DCI. He was a seemingly good inmate, and we gave him trustee status. While mowing the pasture behind my house on state property, he unhooked the bush hog and drove the tractor over to the barn and through the gate. Inmate Fontenot drove the tractor across the pasture by my house and past my car into the woods adjoining the pasture. Thank God he didn't steal my car. He hid the tractor, crossed the fence, and hitched a ride. He rode to the next town, Zachary, and there he stole a late-model white Mercury Marquis. He then bought several cans of red spray paint and painted the car red. You can imagine how the almost-new car looked— pale red with stripes.

"At the time working for me at the prison was Bill Carville (now deceased), brother of the former Clinton advisor James Carville. Bill was one of these guys who could do anything he wanted. He was persistent and relentless when he undertook a task. Bill teamed up with Joe Williams, a local boy who was quite a detective. He had worked with the Chicago Police Department and wanted to come home to Louisiana, so I hired him. Good people help us be successful and look good. I told Bill and Joe that Inmate Fontenot had to be in the Lafayette area. The car had been sighted in that vicinity, and even though it was early fall, I told them to go there and find him or the car, or 'Don't come home until Christmas!' If they located the car, I told them to sit tight and call me.

"About three weeks later I got the call about 8:00 p.m. They had located the car at an apartment complex in Lafayette. I told them to sit tight. Colonel Bub McNeal, Major Reggie Felker, Major Paul Perkins, and I drove as fast as we could the ninety miles to Lafayette. Sure enough, there it was. I thought, What a horrible paint job. The owner is really going to be mad when he sees his car.

"We then went to the Lafayette Police Department, telling them the story. They were anxious to help, so we made a plan. We contacted the manager of the apartment complex, explaining the situation. We determined there were six people in the apartment—four adults and two children. We certainly didn't want a hostage situation, so we planned to stage a fire and scare them out. We evacuated the apartment complex late that night, very quietly. We brought up two large fans and smoke bombs. We arranged for a fire truck to drive up at 4:00 a.m. The fire truck was to blow the loud fire horn—not the siren. We thought the siren might frighten him, and he would take the others hostage or try to escape out the back window. We assumed he probably had a gun, and we didn't want anyone to get hurt. Since Bill Carville and Joe Williams, as well as Colonel McNeal and Major Felker, could recognize him best during the chaos of the perceived 'fire,' they dressed in fire suits, as firemen.

"At 4:00 a.m., all was ready. The fans were turned on, the smoke bombs ignited, and with the smoke blowing toward the door of the apartment (the electric power had been turned off, so it would be virtually dark), the fire truck came driving into the apartment complex. With its loud horn blowing, Bill and Joe ran up to the door, knocking very loudly, shouting, 'FIRE, FIRE! RUN FOR YOUR LIFE! FIRE, FIRE! GET OUT! GET OUT, EVERYBODY—GET OUT!' And they came one after the other, just like squirrels out of a pin oak tree—with the women and children first. Previously escaped Inmate Fontenot was last. He ran right into the arms of Colonel McNeal, and he was 'escaped' no more. One of the women got really mad, and I told her to shut up unless she wanted to be charged with harboring a fugitive. That brought her to reality, and then home we came, to DCI. No more trustee status for Inmate Fontenot. The prisoner got two more years added to his sentence, and Bill Carville and Joe Williams got two weeks off. The Lafayette police did a wonderful job, and the paper later wrote, 'That was a police operation from which movies are made.'"

When it comes to keeping the inmates in, Angola's size is both a blessing and a curse. The expansive acreage permits inmates to enjoy a degree of freedom outdoors. It also means that many of them will have work assignments away from the camps where they eat, sleep, and recreate. The movement of hundreds of prisoners from one point to another throughout the day means there must be a way to account for every prisoner at key junctures. Head counts occur first in the mornings and then later at random, whenever prisoners return to living quarters. Everyone is kept under tight surveillance, movement restricted, until all prisoners are accounted for.

Daily life in prison often becomes a series of hurry-up-and-wait moments for inmates who must travel from one point to another. It is not uncommon for a prisoner who must report to a new workstation, for example, to wind up waiting at a checkpoint until an officer clears him to pass.

Numbers are everything at Angola. The number of inmates must match the total prison population without one variation. Until they do, no one is free to move about. Numbers that do not add up exactly mean one thing: Someone is attempting to escape.

Warden Cain is proud of his chase team, a group of tactical officers whose responsibility is to track down potential escapees. Not many inmates attempt escape—but then again, from the warden's perspective, one escape attempt is one too many. He knows that people living nearby—twenty or so miles outside Angola's main gate—are relying on him to protect them. Anytime an inmate escapes, even for a few hours, amid the glare of frantic publicity, nearby residents may barricade themselves in their houses, fearful that a fleeing inmate might try to break in, steal a car, or, worst of all, take them hostage.

Angola operates in high gear whenever someone flees. The staff keeps prisoners in lockdown within their living units. Most work in the fields and elsewhere across the prison comes to a halt. The camps are carefully searched, as are the barns, maintenance buildings, and other facilities. The chase team is familiar with the potential hiding places on the grounds where inmates might sequester themselves until they sense they can escape.

The prison chase team practices preventive drills. The correctional officers who comprise the team go after a prison employee or two whose goal it is to elude capture for a couple of hours. Warden Cain's own son, Marshall, used to participate with a friend—"they run like inmates run," Cain said, "getting lost and running real crazy, so it was like chasing real prisoners." Assistant Warden Cathy Fontenot, once a college runner, has served as bait for practice chases in the past. Until she became pregnant with her third child, she enjoyed playing hide-and-seek with the chase team. "Sometimes, when we'd burrow into a hillside or under some woody brush, we could hear the officers in the distance as they were searching for us. Once, a couple of them were so close that we could reach out and touch them."

A real chase is no such amusement. The objective is clear—to find the escaping inmate and return him safely, if possible, to Angola. The advantage is with the officers on the chase team. They are armed and equipped with vehicles, including an army surplus amphibious "duck," and they can even solicit the use of a sheriff's helicopter to aid in searching along the edge of the Mississippi River.

The officers also utilize dogs in the chase. The prison has a large dog population composed of bloodhounds, German shepherds, mixed breeds, and even a few part wolves, the latter mostly for show. (Some of the dogs are employed to sniff for illicit drugs in the prison camps.) The dog handlers train the bloodhounds—big, floppy ears, gentle dispositions, and superior scent—to hunt for runaway inmates. They are difficult to distract when they are on the chase and usually ignore the alligators, poisonous snakes, and bears lurking in the woods on the one side of Angola not abutting the Mississippi. Angola's chase dogs are extraordinarily well trained. Their handlers even prepare some dogs for use against escapes in other states.

With respect to keeping peace at Angola, the warden and his staff realize that the men and women who guard inmates have demanding jobs. They must interact with prisoners in a no-nonsense and professional way, signaling that they are in charge, even though they are unarmed. There can be no fraternization between staff and inmates. Physical or verbal abuse is forbidden. Any correctional officer who mistreats inmates under his authority creates a major safety problem for himself and others. Any correctional officer operating solo without approval, ignoring directives and procedures, also undermines Burl Cain's considerable vision to establish a penitentiary where inmates serving long or life sentences can still enjoy a useful existence. The warden is particularly concerned when frontline correctional officers block the passage of information that he and his team are trying to convey to the prisoners.

Yet there are times when force is necessary to control an unmanageable inmate. Whenever possible, a specially trained tactical team administers the force. One team member explains: "We do that so the officers regularly assigned to the area where the problem has occurred are not perceived by the inmates as overly harsh and eager to employ force to restore order. We go in and fix the problem. Then the assigned staff member can step aside while we do the job and come back in without facing a potential backlash from other inmates."

The rule is that the force used can be only one step greater than the inmate's belligerent behavior in his refusal to cooperate. When the inmate stops resisting, then the team ceases the use of force. "The extra lick is the one that gets you sued," Cain remarks. If an inmate won't come out of his cell, for example, the tactical team will go in and extricate him. If he resists in some way—say, for instance, he shoves an approaching team member—the officer can grab the inmate in an armlock or other preventative hold. If the inmate uses a homemade weapon, the officer can respond by swinging a baton, or nightstick, at the man's arm or leg.

On rare occasions, the force to regain control in a perilous situation may be deadly, as it was in the hostage situation when the tactical team followed Warden Cain into an area where a few inmates were holding three correctional officers hostage. Before two of the hostages were released (the third had been killed early on), the team had to fatally shoot one inmate and wound one other.

Most crucially, the warden and his staff must maintain total control. The inmates can never suspect the staff is weak, uncertain, or pliable. They should never believe that they may get away with infractions or bend the rules to suit their purposes. They must always know that the warden and his team will react consistently, appropriately, and with the right degree of force when the situation demands it. Otherwise, the inmates appear to usurp their power and dictate control.

"We have good security, but we're not oppressive," says Cain. "We'd rather be good, because, as I tell the inmates, I'm doing time too, and I want to do good time, not bad time."

At Angola, security shakedown crews operate throughout the prison on a continuous basis. Their inspections are always a surprise, and it is intentional. Finding and confiscating contraband in a prison is a full-time occupation for the staff. Every piece of contraband that remains undiscovered represents an opportunity for an inmate, up to no good, to carry out an insidious scheme, whether to attack a corrections officer or another inmate or perhaps to perpetrate an attempted escape.

One definition of contraband is the possession of an unauthorized item, such as an illegal drug. Another is the possession of an authorized item but for an unauthorized purpose. That was the problem with the missing needle. Using it to sew up burlap feed bags was perfectly acceptable. Having the needle reappear, as a weapon, in a prison dormitory was not.

The shakedown crews are made up of specially trained officers who are assigned to enter the inmates' living quarters while they are out on work assignments. The crews search everything for contraband. They carefully inspect bedding, looking for signs that an inmate has undone a seam in a mattress, for example, to hide a small homemade weapon or a marijuana joint. Consider how one crew member approaches his assignment:

"When I search, I try to envision where I might hide contraband if I was a prisoner. I try to look into the most obscure places where something might be cached. It is amazing to uncover some of the stuff we find in the most unusual places. The inmates are resourceful."

A shakedown crew also sifts through inmate footlockers, inspecting clothing, opening up and shaking out books and magazines, emptying small boxes and packages where inmates store personal items. The officers do not tear up the inmates' living quarters, but neither do they replace everything exactly as the men left their items when they went off to work assignments. Leaving a man's personal belongings a bit out of kilter serves to remind the inmates that their stuff is subject to a search at any time.

In short, when a shakedown crew arrives in a dorm or cell block, everything is going to be searched, and searched carefully. Invariably, a crew finds something that should not there. Then, depending on what has been found, the inmate who tried to hide it could face the disciplinary board and consequent punishment.

An Angola security officer received the tip from an inmate source, one whose identity the officer pledged to protect. The information was clear but scant.

Supposedly, a nurse working in the prison infirmary—a "free person" making her living at Angola—was secretly meeting with an inmate trustee in the early morning hours on weekends. After her shift was over, she would pick him up in her automobile, and they would spend an hour or so together before she would drop him off at his living quarters. The inmate resided in a building where he could slip out between security checks conducted throughout the night by a correctional officer.

In prison, administrators never ignore tips, no matter how outlandish they might seem—because in prison, you never know.

"We get a lot of information on the sly from inmates who hear things through the rumor mill," Warden Cain says. "They tell us because they know that if what they've heard is true, the person or persons involved can jeopardize everyone, not just themselves. We want our inmates to value their everyday lives enough to want to stop someone from upsetting everything by an act that's criminal or violates the rules."

The prison's security staff set up teams to surreptitiously monitor the actions of the nurse and inmate on Friday night. Nothing happened. They repeated the process on Saturday night. At about 3:00 a.m., the nurse's car stopped at the inmate's living quarters, and he slipped out the door and into the vehicle. Security officers followed the car until it stopped again, in the parking lot of a small, obscure area. The officers immediately took the nurse into custody and transported the inmate to Camp J for interrogation.

After a hearing, the inmate lost his trustee status and was sentenced to several months of extended lockdown. The nurse was fired and faced criminal charges in West Feliciana parish.

One incongruity of life at Angola is the small, inauspicious one-story, concrete block building not far from the main camp. Only by entering, there to be greeted by a single officer, does a visitor become aware of the awesome arsenal available to the prison staff. There are pistols, both .45 caliber and 9-millimeter models. There are high-powered rifles and automatic weapons, such as machine guns. There are hand grenades and other explosive devices, including tear gas canisters and stun sticks to incapacitate an unruly inmate. There is even a special body shield that generates sixty thousand volts of electricity to repel an assault.

It's enough firepower for a small army.

Yet with few exceptions, correctional officers do not carry firearms or even batons—otherwise known as nightsticks—at Angola. For one thing, as previously noted, their own weapons might be used against them if inmates overpowered prison staff and seized control of their area. Angola is heavily staffed, but it would be foolhardy to arm the security officers who patrol inside the prison camps. Their most effective "weapons" are two-way radios that keep them in direct contact with security stations. When a problem occurs, the security supervisors quickly can call on additional manpower. Even Warden Cain is linked to his key staff with several two-way radios.

Angola also has a small population of prison workers living on the grounds. A number reside with their families in an area made up of modest single-family homes. Staff members who live in the "B-Line," near Angola's front gate, receive rent-free housing in exchange for being on call around the clock. There is also a two-story apartment complex where single officers reside. They, too, are on call at any hour in the event of an emergency.

Correctional officers are stationed throughout the five prison camps. Some of them, unarmed except for two-way radios, remain on watch inside inmate dormitories overnight. In addition, roving patrols police the property, and the familiar three-story guard towers overshadow the camps. At night, bright spotlights bathe the camps in pale, yellow-orange light, making it next to impossible for an inmate to creep from inside a camp building to the tall fences encircling each complex.

Control of Angola comes in large part by making it clear to the inmates that they cannot challenge the prison's staff without suffering harsh consequences. Yet there also must be an understanding that no one —inmate or security staff—wins if the prison always must be in lockdown mode. There must be an accommodation—an understanding that Angola will not work if the staff must operate as though the prison is always on the verge of insurrection.

A penitentiary that depends primarily on armed guards, inflexible rules, the threat of lethal force, and an implied enthusiasm to crack down at the slightest whim may keep the peace, but at a steep price. Such facilities must establish better methods of control if they are going to make it possible for the many inmates who do go along with the prison program to conduct their lives with minimal disruption.

So the vast arsenal of weapons in that nondescript little building is kept under lock and key. And the peace, mostly, is kept.

CHAPTER 11

THE YES MAN

Burl Cain's job gives him near-dictatorial control over more than five thousand inmates. How they survive, exist, cope with the tedium of life in confinement in a maximum-security prison is up to him. He can make life bearable for the men consigned to Angola. He can introduce, or withhold, programs designed to give them opportunities to make something of themselves, even behind bars. He can give the signal—and has, six times, in a state that allows capital punishment—to send a man to his death on a terrifying gurney in the lonely execution chamber. He can reward and he can punish.

And he can say yes or no.

It is easier for a warden to say no. It takes little mental effort to say no. The answer no means that nothing changes. Change involves risk, even when it is well thought out. Saying no decreases the chance that whatever was being requested might backfire if granted. Yet saying no also means that tension is likely to build up, eventually to a boiling point. When a warden is maintaining the status quo, keeping the lid on, enforcing tight control, and making sure everyone knows that his principal tool to run the place is brutal force, few inmates' lives are likely to improve. Every no increases hostility and frustration.

A no warden may be asked: Can we help inmates who are critically ill face death with dignity, with men who show care and compassion at their sides in those final days? Uh-uh. His rationale: The volunteers may be able to cop some of the drugs used to sedate the dying inmate. A no warden is asked: Can we establish some clubs to help us improve or enjoy our free time? No. His rationale: If the inmates gather socially outside their workday, they're likely to scheme and upset the prison. A no warden is asked: Can we have greater opportunities to sell our crafts and make some spending money during the rodeo? No. His rationale: The inmates shouldn't be benefiting that much financially from the event; keep 'em lean and mean. A no warden is asked: Can we allow our good inmate preachers and gospel bands to go outside the prison, carefully monitored and guarded, and perform in churches across Louisiana? Absolutely not. His rationale: Even the most responsible inmates can't be trusted. If one of them hurts a free person, I'll lose my job.

Burl Cain has another point of view. It has become his hallmark at Angola. "You have to evaluate the risk and then say yes more than no—if the benefit outweighs the risk."

In the ten years he has managed the prison, Cain has worked hard to build a team of key staff members who buy into that philosophy. The enthusiasm for what he is accomplishing is reflected in the remarks of Cathy Fontenot, one of his assistant wardens.

"It's one thing to say that inmates are human. It's another to treat them that way. The warden has taught me how to do that. Our lives are so limited to inconsequential things. The inmates aren't worried about whether they're getting cheese with their Whopper. They want to know, 'Why am I here? What am I going to do tomorrow?'"

Answering those and a host of other questions is what keeps Burl

Cain on his toes. He knows he is always a phone call from disaster. It is the very nature of life in a maximum-security prison like Angola. The knowledge that he could be facing a crisis in the next minute drives Cain to his knees. "I pray for wisdom, and when it comes, I say 'Thank You, Jesus.'"

Here is a seeming contradiction. Burl Cain wields unquestioned power at Angola—and yet openly embraces a personal faith in God and puts that faith into practice whenever he can. How does the warden resolve the tension?

Many people of faith are seen in the workplace as clueless Bible-thumpers who don't understand real life, who try to comfort hurting neighbors and coworkers with misused and clichéd Scripture verses—rather than just wrapping their arms around those hurting people and whispering, "What can I do to help?"

Burl Cain is a committed follower of Christ. Yet he doesn't carry a Bible around the prison grounds. He doesn't spout Bible verses at inappropriate times. He doesn't wear his Christianity on his sleeve. But he listens and he admits when he doesn't have the answers. He doesn't use Bible verses to drive inmates away. He gives them opportunities to explore the real meaning of faith, but it is up to them whether they do. Cain can be earthy when the occasion demands it. He can be tough and demanding. He does not spiritualize issues, or allow others to do so, as an excuse to avoid making decisions that must be made. He is not out to win a popularity contest. When he acts, even when he does something that may anger some staff members as well as the inmates, he rarely agonizes over a decision if he has thought it out thoroughly, as he generally does.

Cain's deep faith does not stop him from taking strong, even harsh actions when the situation requires it.

Cain's approach in dealing with the hostage crisis reflected one of his philosophies as the warden. He determined well before the incident that he would not negotiate with hostage takers; to do so, he believed, would open the door to repeated crises. If prisoners know they can get away with such actions, that the warden will hear, and maybe even accede to, their demands, none of his unarmed security officers will be safe. So when he arrived at the prison camp where his three guards were being held, he issued an ultimatum—give up the hostages and surrender, then we'll talk. When they refused, he took immediate action.

Cain also has pledged to his staff that should any of them ever be taken as hostages, he will do everything in his power to get them out immediately. The warden knows that captors in a prison setting often abuse and torture hostages before killing them when the warden will not meet their demands. He has vowed he will not let that happen—"I will get you out; you will not suffer that kind of mistreatment."

Some inmates also are critical because Cain emphasizes religion as the most effective means of achieving moral rehabilitation. They wonder if that approach is not simply the "flavor of the month."

Yet there is no doubt that Cain's faith has had a huge impact on Angola. It spurred him to negotiate with the seminary that now offers college training to Angola inmates so that, regardless of their religion, they might receive a college degree or become missionaries in other Louisiana prisons. That, in turn, has led to many inmates who are Christians becoming scattered throughout the prison to share their faith by example as well as word. The warden has resisted the impulse to gather all of the Christians in one living area. "How can they have any impact on the prison if the only men they are living with are Christians like themselves?"

The extension seminary has proved to be a major yes program, despite some initial skepticism. Three classes already have graduated, and the seminary has sent more than eighty men into inmate missionary roles at Angola and other Louisiana prisons. Deputy Warden Sheryl Ranatza, who has become the top lieutenant to Burl Cain, explains one reason for the skepticism: "It's hard to change the culture at Angola. It took someone like Warden Cain to make what is becoming a lasting difference here. The statistics speak for themselves. Angola is a much more peaceful place, with incidents of violence, escape, infractions all down significantly. Yet everything the warden does initially meets some resistance. When he began talking about bringing the New Orleans Baptist Theological Seminary here, people said, 'It'll never work.' The notion was really weird from everybody's perspective—except for Warden Cain. Then we had that first graduating class, and then another. And we began to see real change in the culture of the prison."

Cain also moved to develop a hospice program that is linked to the prison's infirmary. Gravely ill inmates can face death with dignity, supported by compassion. Volunteers are at their bedside around the clock, making sure they are not alone as they face their last hours on earth.

The warden has spoken often about a growing issue in most prisons —the rising number of elderly inmates, men who have spent most of their adult lives behind bars. They require more medical care, generally, and they often have no families on the outside who can help them when they become chronically and critically sick. Many of them represent no threat if released—they committed crimes as hotheaded youths. They have long since rejected the out-of-control lives that got them sent to prison.

And as they age behind bars, they will need more medical treatment, at significant cost to the state. The warden believes the cost of keeping increasingly frail, elderly, harmless inmates in prison could be far better spent on the predators who do threaten society. He thinks there may be as many as a couple hundred elderly inmates, some in their seventies and even eighties, who could be set free without any risk to society.

"We need the space for predators, not for dying old men," he has said.

Yet Cain also realizes that the politics of crime are powerful. A governor has to be strong to risk setting free men whom his constituents demanded, through the laws that were passed long ago, should spend their lives in prison. There is, as well, the practical matter of releasing inmates who have no safety net—no support system on the outside to help them cope with newfound freedoms they have not enjoyed for decades. The shocking scene in *The Shawshank Redemption* when Brooks, the elderly prison librarian, finally released, climbs onto a chair in his rented room and hangs himself, is not altogether fiction.

Too often, once a prisoner is let out, he has nowhere to go and little or no prospect for a job. Even the churches that worked with him while he was in prison may abandon him after a brief time. Ex-cons, after all, often are not easy men to help.

But as long as they remain inside, Cain will try to help them—and encourage their "neighbors" to do the same.

In the prison's hospice, volunteers sit alongside men who are dying, providing a bit of companionship as they meet the small, but important, needs of these unfortunate inmates. Listen as Frank Green, a hospice volunteer who received a life sentence for murder, explains why he devotes some of his free time to being with terminal prisoners:

"To me, it's a way to give back, to help somebody in need. Staying with the patients gives them an opportunity to have a familiar face around them, to feel as though somebody genuinely cares. Sometimes the volunteers cry when the patients cry. I cry within me—I don't want my tears to seem fake."

Green admits he sometimes becomes attached to a patient. It is hard when the man's final hours of life are slipping away. When that time comes, the prison administration allows a half-dozen hospice volunteers to be released from their normal prison jobs to conduct a bedside vigil.

And when the end does come, they are carried on an antique hearse replica, pulled by huge Percheron draft horses and built by inmates, to the prison cemetery, where their friends can inter them with dignity. That, too, was Burl Cain's idea.

Gang activity is a constant danger in prisons. Cain has come to realize he can block gang activity—that in reality often is an inmate's way of finding something to which he can belong—by establishing many other ways for the men to belong, to find purpose and meaning. Recently, Joni and Friends, an organization that reaches out to physically disabled persons, approached the warden with a proposal he found irresistible. Through its Wheels for the World program, the ministry has access to hundreds of broken-down wheelchairs donated by supporters. Would the inmates at Angola have an interest, the ministry's president asked, in refurbishing those wheelchairs so they could be donated to handicapped people living in Third World nations? (It is easier to ship wheelchairs to other countries than make them available in the United States because of product liability lawsuits that might crop up if a refurbished chair does not meet exact operating standards.)

Cain took the proposition to the heads of the prison's inmate clubs, describing to them how disabled individuals in poor countries have to be dragged around on blankets if they want to have any mobility. "Some of them had tears in their eyes as I told that story," he says.

They endorsed the idea enthusiastically. He and his staff then determined that the project could be housed in the same area where abandoned bicycles are rebuilt and given as gifts to needy kids across Louisiana. The staff also identified a number of trustee inmates it could select to set up a procedure and assume responsibility for refurbishing the wheelchairs. Within weeks, the first broken-down wheelchairs began arriving at Angola. Eventually 160 wheelchairs a month will find their way to the poor people on the blankets.

"We accomplish a lot when we take on a program like this," the warden says. "We help people who need help. We show the outside world that our men are interested in making a contribution to bettering the lives of others. And our men gain a sense of real achievement. It is a win-win in the best sense."

Angola prisoners have donated $15,000 to the American Red Cross for families of the victims of the September 11, 2001 terrorist attacks, as well as contributing $2,500 for Asian tsunami relief early in 2005. Recently inmates sent a container load of medical equipment to Tanzania. Inmates and staff collected the equipment, cleaned it up, and loaded the container for shipping to Africa. The program, sponsored by the American Correctional Association under the leadership of Dr. Betty Gondles, is another way men who seemingly have nothing—men who have committed tragically selfish acts—are changing and learning to help others.

CHAPTER 12

"I DIDN'T DO IT"

The color photographs on top of the metal file cabinet show the faces of smiling, attractive young adults. They were taken while they were in college. Kerry Myers displays the photos with justifiable pride, and he readily shares with a visitor what his now-grown children have accomplished during the fifteen years he has been in prison. The cabinet is behind Myers's desk in a small office inside the main prison camp at Angola. He spends most of his days working out of that office as editor of the *Angolite*. Although he concentrates on his prison job, putting out a publication that reaches many outside Angola, Myers can turn in his chair to admire those photos.

Myers sees his children on occasion, when they find time, all too rarely, to visit him in prison. He tries to impart whatever wisdom he can during those brief meetings in the noisy visitors' area and in long, crafted letters that this inmate journalist writes and sends to them. Myers cherishes the correspondence and photos he gets from them. His children remain a vital, yet distant, link with the world beyond the prison's grounds. Myers would give anything to see them regularly, although he recognizes that it is not likely to happen—ever.

It becomes clear in what amounts to a wisp of conversation with the inmate that Myers, like so many prisoners at Angola, is frustrated. He cannot ease a pain that is so agonizingly deep inside him, a pain that never seems to depart. Myers is frustrated, and he must keep that frustration under control. He has missed every occasion when his children did something special, whether bringing home an outstanding report card, winning an athletic contest, or just sharing the joy of youth.

He is serving a life sentence without parole, and winning a pardon is an uphill battle, at best, no matter how good he is at Angola.

Even if the state pardon board members were to consider and then recommend Myers for release in the future, he still might not leave prison before he is an old man. By then, his children may have raised families of their own, and their father may have great difficulty reconnecting to their lives this late. Their love for him, dimmed by long years of separation, may never be rekindled beyond a frail spark.

Yet one other issue frustrates Kerry Myers more than all others. No one, so far, has taken him seriously when he proclaims—in a calm voice, beginning almost apologetically with the phrase "you won't want to hear this"—that he is innocent.

Most prisoners at Angola do not freely discuss the crimes they committed. They answer but without providing any details. Few will argue that they were wrongly convicted, although some maintain they expected lesser sentences when they pleaded guilty. They may claim their attorneys misled them into believing the judge would give them a limited-term sentence of, say, ten or fifteen years. Now they are locked up for life, and no one seems to care about the injustice they believe was done to them.

Kerry Myers is the rare inmate who maintains his innocence. But, while he searches for justice, he is making a life, trying to build something of value.

It is, unfortunately, a near-impossible task to talk with every inmate who has a good story to tell. That would take years. In essence, the decision to concentrate on a relative handful of men is based on the belief that there are recurrent themes to their stories. Each did something awful to wind up in prison, most felt the cold chill and fear as they entered the gates to Angola. Each struggled to maintain dignity in the early days in prison as they warded off predators seeking to take advantage. Some rebelled at first, then found something—often faith—to open their eyes at last and cause them to change their ways. Each now has found his place in a unique community, contributing to its betterment. Each still hopes, someday, to be free again. Some admit the likelihood of winning a parole or pardon would be a miracle.

The interviewer chooses carefully, then, to select the men with whom he will talk. Yet at the same time he realizes his selection of interviewees must of necessity be haphazard. There are too many good stories, and he knows he is missing many. What does become part of the story about Angola—the thumbnail sketches of a handful of inmates—is not meant as a contrived or misguided attempt to build empathy for these men. It would be foolish to paint altogether sympathetic word pictures of inmates who are in prison, after all, for what they have done.

Yet the interviewer cannot help but be impressed as he listens to these inmates. In their stories, one sees the completion of Warden Burl Cain's thrust to help these men achieve moral rehabilitation. They have looked into the mirror and decided they do not like what they see. Rather than smashing the mirror and continuing down paths toward perversity and destruction, they have cleaned themselves up, starting deep down, on the inside, where it really counts. They have taken responsibility for the acts that got them to Angola. They have chosen to reshape their lives, to become the person whom they might have developed into on the outside had they not gotten into trouble.

Now, when they stare into that mirror, they see a new creation and they like what they see.

You already have met the Bishop—Eugene Tanniehill, the preeminent inmate preacher at Angola. His is the story of how much God can change a man's heart. Others you will meet also have experienced that kind of rehabilitation. Some, however, have not to the degree, at least, that the Bishop so openly professes. Even so, they have found a rudder they can use to keep them on a steady course.

❦

Kerry Myers has spent much of his adult life at Angola. Now middle-aged, he is compactly built yet has a slight paunch. His face is clean shaven except for a neatly trimmed mustache. His dark hair is close cropped at the sides but full and wavy on top. He wears a gray T-shirt and blue jeans, standard prison garb, yet one can almost picture him in another setting, wearing a white dress shirt, offsetting tie, and dark, conservative business suit, totally at ease working in a business office.

He does not smile easily. When you are in prison, the events that bring laughter and joy to those on the outside do not exist. It is not a happy environment, even in the best of circumstances.

An inmate talking with a visitor, or submitting to an interview, does not know quite how open to be. He does not know if his words may come back to haunt him. He has no reason to trust his questioner who, after all, is on the prison grounds for only a few days before returning to the comforts of his free world.

The impressions of Kerry Myers come, then, from observing him as he answers a few questions and discusses, briefly and without complaint, the challenges of putting out a prison newsmagazine on a schedule that may become erratic for any number of reasons.

Prison time is slow time. A key prison staff member, serving as publisher, reviews all stories in the *Angolite*. That takes time. The print shop has other priorities and has to fit the newsmagazine into its production schedule. There was a fire at one point, and the *Angolite* offices moved to a new location.

Myers and each *Angolite* staff member must be Class A trustees who can travel around the prison grounds to develop stories and take photographs. The men recognize their conduct must remain beyond reproach.

The job, their daily assignment, is to produce the newsmagazine. It is carried out in small, yet comfortable, quarters in the main prison camp, with computers, desks, and even a TV monitor to catch news and opinion programs. No correctional officer peers over the staff's collective shoulder to make sure they are cranking away.

At one point recently, more than a year had passed between editions, and Myers was getting heat about picking up the pace. He noted that his staff of five writers, editors, and photographers was rushing to get back on schedule. The *Angolite* is not a puff piece, and the staff takes pride in its work. The publication's high profile among journalists on the outside, largely acquired as the result of a former editor's outspoken and sometimes abrasive writings, allows Myers and his inmate journalists to function somewhat independently, even while being held strictly accountable for what appears in the publication. Most articles pass muster without being censored from above, even when the subject matter may be sensitive. The *Angolite* enjoys a reputation for candid coverage of critical national issues involving the death penalty and incarceration. Some say that if you want to know what inmates are thinking across the land, the place to find out is the *Angolite*. The men on its staff are dedicated to excellence in their writings and photographs. They share the analytical, yet critical, demeanor so common among journalists. Ask a question, and they respond with a question in return. They are respectful to a "free" journalist who stops into the *Angolite* office, yet he quickly recognizes that their carefully chosen comments nonetheless have the edgy quality of a subtle grilling.

An *Angolite* staff member's biggest concern is that he will somehow lose his trustee status. Any failure of conduct that results in forfeiting trustee status means automatic removal from the *Angolite* staff, since the writers, editors, and photographers must enjoy enough freedom to travel unaccompanied across the prison grounds as they develop stories.

What makes Kerry Myers particularly intriguing is his insistence—in a flat yet convincing tone—that he did not commit the crime that got him sent to Angola for life. He was convicted of engineering the killing of his wife. As Myers describes the case, parallels to the popular movie and earlier TV series *The Fugitive* come to mind. When his wife's murder occurred, police first arrested another man. He was tried but freed when the jury could not reach a unanimous verdict. The case remained unsolved until the police rearrested the original defendant.

This time the man claimed that Myers hired him to commit the killing. The state tried both men for murder. The alleged actual killer got a limited sentence; he's out now. Myers insisted from the very beginning that he had nothing to do with the death of his children's mother. The jury didn't believe him. Immediately, he lost everything he had built up, starting with his freedom. Most of all, he lost all meaningful contact with his kids.

Hearing Myers's claim, the first thought that crossed an interviewer's mind was that were he innocent—yet locked away forever—he would spend every waking moment yelling at the top of his lungs that he had been framed.

Myers does not scream or shout about what has made him a prisoner at Angola, perhaps forever. "I didn't do it," he says simply as he leans back in his chair at the *Angolite* office. "I didn't kill my wife. I loved her. Someday, maybe I'll finally have the opportunity to prove it."

Then his voice trails off. "For now . . ."

With that, Myers turns his attention again to the task at hand, preparing the next edition of his magazine for publication. A prison official accompanying the interviewer as he talked with Myers later agreed that the *Angolite* editor could well be innocent: "I wouldn't be surprised if he got out someday."

In the chapter that follows, the reader can see how other men arrived at Angola after committing terrible acts, how they overcame the initial shock of having to live in a maximum-security prison, and how they chose to make the best of their lives in what some might describe as their community. Whatever you call it, their decisions to make the most of Angola fall under the category of moral rehabilitation. Although they may remain here until they die, they are different—vastly different—men now. Society does them a disservice when it continues to describe those who are truly morally rehabilitated as predators, animals, and killers. They are inmates, prisoners, and lifers for sure. But, most of all, they are men trying to redeem their time on this prison farm as best they can.

CHAPTER 13

IN FOR LIFE, MAKING A LIFE

Randy Ellis

Randy Ellis first met Burl Cain thirteen years ago, when he was serving a term at Dixon Correctional Institution, a medium-security facility about thirty miles from Angola. Cain was Dixon's warden, a position he held for thirteen years before taking over the Louisiana State Penitentiary. As a trustee, Ellis worked at the Dixon horse stable and on flower beds around the warden's home on the prison grounds. Ellis and Marshall Cain, the warden's then-young son, soon became fast friends. They used to race around on the warden's property on motorized scooters and fight each other with BB guns. During an escape, Cain told Ellis to guard the warden's home: "I had an inmate guarding my house!" he laughs now.

After seven and a half years at Dixon, Ellis got out, but soon he lost his freedom again. Six weeks into his freedom, he got drunk and was sentenced to life for second-degree murder, stabbing a cousin to death. (Cain comments that liquor is just as bad as drugs in many ways: "Drugs make you crazy. Liquor makes you mad.")

His sentence landed him in Angola. "I used to pray I wouldn't ever wind up at Angola. The prison had a real bad reputation. I was surprised how nice the prison was."

Ellis comes from a family of six children—three brothers and two sisters. His father, called "Bluegill," died when Randy was still incarcerated at Dixon. His mother lives in his hometown of Haynesville, Louisiana, and he hasn't seen her. "She can't afford to travel here. I talk to her on the telephone."

One brother is also at Angola. Jimmy Ellis, also serving life for second degree murder, has had a hard life in prison. He once tried to kill himself, and now he is housed in a single cell in a special unit for emotionally disturbed inmates. "He didn't want to be in the general population of the prison," Randy said. "It's not that he wants to hurt anybody. He just does better in TU (the special unit)."

Ellis did not know at first that Burl Cain was now in charge of the maximum-security prison. Nor did the warden become aware that Ellis had been sentenced again and was now at Angola. "I transferred him up to the Ranch House (a comfortable facility used to entertain guests) as soon as I found out," Cain said. Ellis does maintenance work at the guest facility as well as at a cottage on the hill overlooking the prison where guests stay overnight.

Ellis said he loves the warden like a father. "He's been good to me. This is one of the best places to do time if you have to do time."

Randy recalled that his brother, who has been at Angola for a long time, once described the prison as a frightful place. "He told me that he used to tie a book on his chest when he went to sleep so no one could stab him. Now you could have a twelve-year-old come here and he'd be safe."

Now in his early forties, Ellis has developed a serious illness, one that ultimately could take his life. "My kidneys went out on me some months ago. I go to Dixon for dialysis treatments three times a week for four hours at a crack." The state does not cover the costs of transplant surgery for inmates serving life sentences. Even though he may be physically eligible for a kidney transplant, the likelihood is that Ellis will never get one since his family would have to pay for it.

He does not expect to be released.

A.J. Freeman

It was Monday night, and there was a worship service in the visitors' room at the main camp. The gospel band had already begun to warm up the crowd of fifty or more inmates who came to worship and enjoy the fellowship. They sang boisterously as the band's vocalists led them through upbeat Southern gospel songs.

One band member was missing; the sweet licks from his electric guitar were silent, the low-keyed, muted accompaniment that so filled in the gaps was missing. A.J., the guitar player, had been called from the room. Word quickly spread that his mother had died, and the chaplain was breaking the sad news to him this very moment. No one expected A.J. to return that night. "The sorrow of his loss has to be overwhelming," someone whispered.

Yet in a few minutes, the guitarist threaded his way past men now standing along the walls of the crowded room, sat down at his place in the band, and began to play as though nothing had happened. Only his downward gaze hinted at the extent of his emotional pain. Soon inmates were coming up to him, patting him on the shoulders, hugging him as he strummed the guitar, and praying softly into his ear.

"It meant so much to me," Oscar "A.J." Freeman said later when asked about that night. "The gospel band supports each other. They helped me get through it."

Freeman said he had not seen his mother since 1989. She had deep psychological problems, and she wouldn't come to Angola by herself. So A.J. would call her, and she'd accept the collect calls. "I always told her I loved her." The victim of a heart attack, his mother died at the age of seventy. He went to the funeral. As an inmate trustee, he could attend without having to be shackled and guarded closely by a correctional officer. Still he was devastated. "You can't ever be prepared for your mama's death."

A.J., a native of New Orleans, is in his early forties and has been at Angola since 1987. He was sentenced to life for a murder that he committed under the influence of drugs and alcohol. The combination made him "paranoid," he said. Though he spent fourteen months in a parish jail awaiting trial and then sentencing, Freeman wasn't prepared for Angola.

"I was lost. It was scary coming here. I had to learn the hard way. I had to come to realize that you have to be yourself, not act like someone you're not, to find your way in prison."

A.J. said his father spent five years at Angola in the 1960s, yet imparted no worldly wisdom from that experience to the son. "He never sat me down and explained to me that if you do this, if you commit a bad crime, you will wind up here. When I got convicted, my mama kept repeating, 'I told you so, I told you so.' I rode the prison bus up here, and that was the last time I saw her."

He became a Christian at Angola. "There's no hope but Jesus. I've seen a lot of guys claim that they've changed in here. They get involved in hobbies and other 'good stuff,' but they can't be nothing without Jesus." But he admits that he needs the gospel band "to keep me in line. Music keeps me out of trouble."

Playing in the band is a sidelight for A.J. As a trustee, he gets up every morning at 3:30 to work in the scullery. But the job doesn't interfere with his music.

He learned to play the guitar in prison and became good enough that he was invited to join the Pure Heart Messengers, Angola's main inmate traveling gospel band. He gets to travel outside the penitentiary whenever the band is invited to play at churches and programs in Louisiana. He has even been to the governor's mansion for a concert. That experience impressed him because he saw a "self-flushing toilet and faucets that turn on and off by themselves."

A.J. does not expect to ever win release from prison, where he is serving a life sentence. "I'm not going to base my life on people. That's not reality. I don't have faith in man. I have faith in Jesus. A pardon is a joke. I face reality; man is not going to let me out. I'm prepared to be here forever. If you stay away from all the mess, you can make it."

He would like to see his daughter, now in her early twenties. He hasn't seen her since she was twelve. His daughter has a small daughter now, his only grandchild. "She's apparently a Tasmanian devil," he laughs. "I'm going to try to get my daughter, sister, and others to know that Jesus is the answer. I'm trying to witness to my family to show them the love of Jesus."

A.J. said he has seen Angola change, particularly under the current warden. "The living conditions were nasty when I came here. Burl Cain in his way is trying to reconstruct a lot of stuff—the prison is cleaner now; there are no roaches. More than that, he's trying to establish a better environment. He's a man of God, and I respect that."

Ron Hicks

When he smiles, Ron Hicks positively beams. That smile spreads from his forehead to the small goatee on his chin. The light in his eyes accentuates the words that he speaks about his faith and God's love. It is hard to believe at first that Hicks committed murder as a youth, and that he may never leave Angola. He has not allowed his condition as an inmate serving a life sentence to destroy his joy. The smile is contagious, and the power of his preaching has allowed him to become the pastor of a thriving inmate church with 150 members.

Now in his mid-thirties, Hicks came to Angola at the age of nineteen. Like many inmates at Angola, he began a treacherous journey as a teenager that led him to personal destruction. By the time he killed someone, he already had a four-year-old daughter. She is now approaching twenty. He sees her about four times a year.

Hicks blames no one but himself for what he did that got him sent to Angola. "I gave my heart to Jesus when I was fifteen years old. I went to a tent revival, and I walked with Jesus until I was sixteen. But then I got in with the wrong friends. I began living on the negative side of life. My family tried to instill values in me, but I didn't take heed of them. I didn't do the things I was supposed to do. I'm responsible for the choices I made in my life."

His first day in prison was a shock.

"I was real cold in my feelings—I knew my mother didn't prepare me for this. Even up to the day I arrived here, I was expecting God to deliver me. I see now that God in His wisdom and knowledge allowed me to come here."

At Angola, Hicks began to take advantage of programs that helped him to reestablish the faith he had set aside when he began to hang out with people who influenced him in bad ways. First he took "Experiencing God," a course designed to help people apply biblical principles so they can know and do the will of God. Millions across the globe have used "Experiencing God" materials to achieve closer, more intimate relationships with God. Hicks began to see that God could and would use him despite what he had done.

Next, Hicks enrolled in the pilot program launched at Angola by the New Orleans Baptist Theological Seminary. The seminary already had been engaged in an outreach to inmates at the prison when Burl Cain became warden in 1995. "In '95 we lost our college Pell grant funding," Cain recalls. "I was sitting at the Ranch House with the Rev. T. W. Terrell of the Judson Baptist Association and Dr. George Roundtree, and I was complaining about having no higher education. 'I'll bet I could get New Orleans Baptist Seminary to come here and set up a college,' Rev. Terrell said. 'I can't believe they'd come to Angola,' I said. 'I believe they would,' he said."

And they did. Seminary leaders approached him about setting up an extension program, where inmates could take college-level courses and earn degrees. Cain readily agreed and set aside space for seminary classrooms and offices. Hicks became one of the first graduates of the program in 1999. He ignored the skeptics, who felt the seminary wouldn't last.

"At first folks thought the seminary was just 'Warden Cain's thing'— that it would pass when the novelty wore off. But then, after it kept on going, they realized it was here to stay."

Hicks credits the warden for establishing an atmosphere where an inmate's faith can be expressed openly. "He's strongly influenced those of us who serve as prison pastors and chaplains to do what we need to do."

Besides serving as pastor for one of several churches established at Angola, he also has taught courses in the prison's extension seminary and teaches faith-based classes for prisoners who can't participate, for one reason or another, in the program. He has an office in a multifaith chapel building on the grounds of the main prison camp.

Hicks knows that the prisoners closely observe those who claim to follow Jesus to see if their words and actions are consistent. "Everybody watches everybody else here—they're looking to see whether you're a fake, whether you say one thing and do another. People here can tell when you're living right or not. Everybody's watching when you say you're a Christian.

"I've worked hard to be faithful, to live according to the Word of God, to mature in my life, but I can't say I haven't made mistakes or grown weary—I have. The biggest challenge I have is dealing with failure. When I came here, I thought I had failed in life. I think I could have been successful on the outside. Instead, when I killed someone, I failed my family, my parents, my daughter."

Yet God, Hicks said, has protected him; more than that, he said, God has "really blessed me. I've never had anyone test me as far as my manhood. He saved me. I am somebody. Even though I'm locked up, I'm free —free in my heart and free to be what God wants me to be."

As a prison pastor, Hicks works hard to reach out to other inmates, to show them that God loves them. "If I'm going to be on God's side, I've got to love everybody, particularly those who the world considers unlovable. Some people at Angola don't think that you can become born again in prison, that inmates can actually change. But then they begin to see the difference in men committed to Jesus, and they begin to become more open to hearing what the Bible says about God."

Hicks said he protects his integrity by keeping himself accountable to other Christian inmates and praying with them three times a week. He has seen a real transformation in Angola in recent years. "It's peaceful in here. Men are openly going to church. They're openly carrying Bibles. They walk without fear and without rejection. I think revival's here. God is up to something, and we're a part of it."

Yet Hicks still hopes someday to leave Angola. The grandmother of the young man he killed came to see him and forgave him for what he did. He believes she would not oppose his release from prison someday. "I'm becoming eligible to apply for a pardon (a prisoner must serve fifteen years of a sentence to apply). I know God saved me for a purpose. I still trust God will bring me out . . ."

He would become a pastor if he gets out, Hicks said, mentioning two former Angola inmates who are serving at "free churches." For now, he finds solace in comparing himself to the apostle Paul, who wrote much of what is now the New Testament while serving as a prisoner.

Gary Shaw

Two Class A trustees are assigned to cook meals at the Ranch House. It is a plum assignment, with time to spare when there are not visitors on the grounds and the warden is out of town. The cooks have the opportunity to mix with guests at the prison, some of whom are notable personalities and politicians. The two men are selected as much for their ability to fit in as they are for their culinary talent. Their records at Angola must be nearly flawless. They address guests as "sir" and "ma'am" and go out of their way to make visitors feel at home.

The cooks work closely with the warden, who maintains a friendly, yet distant, professional relationship with both men. Burl Cain manages to hold down the invisible barrier separating him from each cook—who is, after all, a life inmate—while still maintaining an equally invisible keep-your-distance line over which they dare not cross. He gets the "pick of the litter," so to speak, men whose conduct at Angola has been exemplary and who may someday achieve what every inmate desires, a pardon from the governor. Yet no one who comes on board as a cook at the Ranch House has any assurance such a golden opportunity may ever occur.

Meet one of the cooks—Gary Shaw, serving a term of ninety-nine years for armed robbery and five years as an "accessory after the fact" during a murder. That means, without a pardon, he will never get out of Angola. Now in his early thirties, Shaw came to the prison in 1994. His codefendant also is an inmate at Angola. He got hooked on gambling and began robbing people to get money for his "fix." Shaw and the codefendant were charged with killing someone in the course of a holdup that went bad. The judge sentenced him harshly, believing Shaw had pulled the trigger, even though the other man eventually admitted, as Shaw had claimed all along, that he was the actual killer.

Shaw, bespectacled, is a husky, blond-headed man with a warm smile and engaging manner. He is philosophical about his situation even while claiming that his defense attorney misled him into pleading guilty to the charges. "He told me I'd get out in ten to twelve years if I said I did it. Then I pleaded. The judge gave me 104 years, and my attorney disappeared. I'm still hoping to find someone to review my case and lodge an appeal."

He still hopes to get some judge to review his sentence and find it to be cruel and excessive. Yet Shaw knows that may not occur. "You can't ask for justice. You have to ask for mercy."

When he came to Angola, he was scared. "My first day was very depressing. I got put in extended lockdown (a small cell). They put me on an antidepressant, even though I wasn't mentally ill. They didn't know how to deal with me at first."

Soon, though, Shaw went to a working cell block and spent his days on the farm wielding a "swing blade," one of those tools used to chop out weeds and underbrush. He moved into a dormitory and kept out of trouble. Before he was thirty, he had become a trustee, and then a Class A trustee, the highest rank an inmate can achieve at Angola. "I became the second-youngest Class A trustee ever at the prison."

He has been a cook at the Ranch House for more than a year. He worked alongside a man Cain calls one of his favorite inmates—"Big Lou," Louis Cruz, another inmate serving life, now on the cooking staff at the governor's mansion. Shaw hopes to join his friend there someday. Big Lou is urging him to learn to bake, a skill Shaw's mentor insists is necessary for those preparing meals for the governor and her guests.

In the meantime, Shaw is redeeming the time. He not only serves as one of the warden's cooks but also has become an exceptional craftsman. He takes chunks of wood, usually small trunks from dead trees. Then he planes one section smooth and draws, then etches wildlife creations onto the wood. Sometimes, he also mounts small, dead wildlife, like ducks, to the wood chunks, using forms he purchases from outside distributors. Shaw turns out his wood art quickly and is one of the top sellers at the prison's rodeo in April and October. Some of his proceeds go to buy more supplies for his creations. But he also is generous—he donates part of his earnings to other inmates who do not have the skills to attract "free people" buyers to their crafts.

"I've learned a lot about myself since coming to Angola. I don't have to impress others or do things to draw attention to myself. Hobbies have become my outlet now. Before I came to Angola, I was trying to run away from my mistakes. Being here, oddly enough, gives all of us a lot of opportunities—you've just got to find them. It really comes down to what you want to do with your life—there's the rodeo and crafts and trade schools and the seminary. The Bible school (seminary) offers men who attend a $20,000 education."

Shaw credits Warden Cain for much of the turnaround at Angola. "Working for him is kind of hard. He's got a job to do, and you know he's not going to do everything you want him to do. Yet he can be very supportive, and he'll stop and talk to anyone. He's the alpha male, for sure, and everybody is aware of that. Is he fair? Absolutely. Is he tough? Yes, when he has to be. He wants us to be our brother's keeper. Angola is like a house, a big house. He wants us to feel as though this is our home, because it is, no matter how we feel about how we came here."

Most of all, Shaw credits the warden for the cook's position he holds at the Ranch House. "He believed in me. I couldn't even boil eggs when I came up here. Yet he stuck with me even when I had doubts; he gave me honest opinions about what I was doing. He told me when my food was good and when it was bad. So far, it has been good more often than it has been bad."

Brian Dietrich

For Brian Dietrich, one of the most important lessons after coming to Angola was to ignore the men around him who wanted to fool with his mind. "People will tell you what you want to hear to get what they want from you."

His first few days in prison were "a volatile cocktail." He didn't know whom he could trust and he had to endure taunts, some challenging his manhood. "I didn't fully understand the world I was going into. Everything messed with my mind at first. Not being accepted by other prisoners was a demon that I had to deal with."

An inmate's rudest awakening at Angola usually does not come until he has finished his first few weeks or months in a special prison holding area, and he now is assigned to one of the prison's camps for housing. For the first time, he begins to interact with prisoners already familiar with life at Angola and not at all reticent about playing mind games with a new man.

Listen as Dietrich, a native of Baton Rouge who came to Angola seventeen years ago, describes his first few minutes walking into Camp C, his assigned "residence" after indoctrination:

"I was shook. Someone called out, 'You're for me.' Someone else told me I was a 'fresh fish.'"

The comments, with obvious sexual connotations, were meant to unhinge Dietrich, in his early twenties, and they did at first. "It took awhile before I got mentally balanced so that I could understand the world I was going into."

At first Dietrich chose to meet the demands others made of him, because he believed it would make his transition into prison life easier. He eventually realized that he would never adjust if he continued to succumb to the pressures of those around him. He began to blend in, to make his own way.

"Someone told me you have to show people you can do time by yourself . . . that you need no one else. That's what I started to do."

Still, though, for a number of years the inmate fought the system—sneaking marijuana and gambling. Whenever he got caught, he faced administrative lockdown—the so-called "dungeon," Camp J, where recalcitrant inmates are sent to straighten out. The amount of time that an inmate spends in Camp J, in a solitary cell, often unable even to communicate with others in other cells on the same floor, is entirely up to him. Extended lockdown is designed not to punish but rather to persuade inmates to accept what is expected of them in prison. They have the opportunity to show, by their behavior in Camp J, that they are ready to return to a less restrictive environment, in another of Angola's prison camps. Dietrich hated extended lockdown, but he had no emotional resolve to avoid doing the things that got him sent to Camp J in the first place. But something did happen, and it changed his life.

Now in his late thirties, Dietrich continues to serve a life term for second-degree murder. The men who come to Angola are not dragged into prison totally unprepared for what they will face. Most, like Dietrich, already have spent years in some form of incarceration, at the least waiting in a parish jail until their trials. He was in custody for two years before his trial on charges of armed robbery and before authorities matched his fingerprints in the murder case. After conviction, he was taken to Hunt Correctional Institution for two weeks. That's where prisoners are evaluated before assignment at Angola and other Louisiana prisons.

For years, Dietrich experienced an awful existence at Angola. He got in with the wrong crowd, misused drugs, and gambled. Finally, he failed a drug test—the prison staff, equipped with drug-sniffing dogs, keeps close tabs on drug infractions. And he went to Camp J.

In the mid-1990s, Dietrich faced considerable private turmoil in his life. "It was a low time for me. I had thoughts of suicide. My grandfather—my closest link to the outside—told me that if I went to the dungeon, he'd stop visiting me." It was while he was in administrative lockdown that Dietrich became a Christian. "I've seen God's grace in my life. Since becoming a Christian, I haven't smoked a joint or gambled. I have become stabilized."

In his years at Angola, he has seen major changes. "It's much safer. The warden has put his foot down. He's established guidelines, and he expects us to follow them. The guards are respectful; they treat you in a professional manner. You can make a life for yourself in here. The churches have blossomed inside, and lots of guys are trying to seek peace. Warden Cain wants the inmates to have spiritual peace. He says even if you can't go home now, you can go home later—to heaven. Some people think he's just trying to yoke us up, so we cooperate. But he really wants us to have peace."

Dietrich said he does not intend to apply for the seminary at Angola. He does not see his role as a inmate missionary or pastor. "The seminary is for men called to preach. I don't feel I have been called to preach." He works in tractor repair. Dietrich chuckles as he shares advice another inmate in his shop gave him: "If it doesn't work, you need to curse it a little bit."

He knows that the murder he committed took more than his freedom. "I'm still a bit childish. I've never been married. I have a lack of responsibility. I have no children to raise. Without faith, it would be easy to lose hope."

Still he hopes that someone will look at his changed life someday and at the amount of time he has served at Angola and say, "Enough is enough." He hopes, as do many inmates, that then he will go free.

Lane Nelson

He was heading from California to Florida in 1981 to visit his sick mother when Lane Nelson got into the trouble that would send him to Angola for life. He was hitchhiking when a "large woman" picked him up in her car. It turned out "she" was a "he," a transvestite, and Nelson killed the man and then took his car to complete the trip. He was arrested before he ever got to Florida.

Nelson, now in his early fifties, originally was sentenced to death—the crime became first-degree murder when he stole his victim's auto. He wound up on Death Row at Angola. At one point during his two and a half years on the row, eight men were executed in eleven weeks. "I felt sorry for those guys." But he never gave up hope and he kept fighting legally for a reduction in sentence.

"I never did get to see my mom. She passed away three days after I got arrested. At first in jail I planned to kill myself. Then I heard about Jesus from other prisoners, and I knew I had changed when I hadn't said a cussword after I woke up."

He worked hard to redeem the time he spent on Death Row. "I was never bored on Death Row. I read the Bible front to back six or seven times. And I did some writing," including about four hundred articles for a church newsletter.

His next seven years at Angola were spent in a single cell. "I hadn't seen the stars in seven years. When I got transferred to a dormitory to live, I was dizzy at first having all that freedom." Now Nelson is on the staff of the *Angolite,* has coauthored one book, an anthology dealing with the death penalty, and has another book in the works, a portrait of prison life. But his passion is now volunteering at Angola's hospice. He credits Warden Cain with improving the prison's medical care programs, expanding the rodeo, and encouraging the growth of the seminary and religious services.

Nelson helps dying prisoners cope with their last days. At Angola, he says, the word *hospice* stands for Helping Others Share Their Pain Inside a Correctional Environment. There are thirty-six hospice volunteers—inmates who use some of their spare time to show compassion to the handful of inmates with terminal illnesses. The volunteers must be trained and spend thirty hours studying to participate in the program. They must have been free from drugs for five years. Nelson finds satisfaction in hospice work. "It's good to be able to be responsible, to be compassionate. Compassion is the key to change." He has dabbled in Buddhism as well as Christianity.

Articulate and somewhat skeptical, the slight, bespectacled Nelson embraces the journalist's creed. "The pen is mightier than the sword. I use the pen to make things happen."

Nelson still hopes to get out of Angola and has an attorney representing him. He said the pardon board unanimously recommended him for a pardon in 1993 but the then-governor denied him, he believes, because the *Angolite* had criticized the official. The pardon recommendation lapsed when the man left office.

He believes he has earned his freedom from prison. Yet he also admits, "I was very irresponsible when I came to Angola. If I hadn't killed that man, I had a rich aunt in Montana who was going to send me to college."

Billy Fallon

He is young, in his twenties, and he has spent about four years at Angola. Prison officials will tell you that inmates like Billy Fallon can be among the most difficult to handle because they have not been incarcerated long enough to have accepted that society has put them away for their natural lives. Some of these men will try to escape, believing they can somehow elude Angola's vaunted chase team. Others will fit into the crowd of predators who prey on weaker inmates.

Fallon, sentenced to life for second-degree murder, is a student in the seminary program and works as a clerk for the prison chaplain. He spent three and a half years in a parish jail awaiting trial. After conviction he came to Angola after a brief evaluation period at another Louisiana penitentiary. For seven and a half months, before transferring to a dormitory, he lived in a working cell block, sharing a small cell with another inmate, and toiled in the farm field.

He pulled out his prison identification card and handed it to the interviewer. When the photo was taken on his first day at Angola, Fallon was sporting a mustache (now shaved), had no eyeglasses on (he wears them now), and was dressed in a white uniform (in the seminary, he dresses comfortably in a white T-shirt and state-issued blue jeans).

He admits he made a real mess of his life before coming to prison. He liked to pretend he was a Mafia killer or another kind of "macho-type person." He wanted people to fear him. He committed acts that totally contradicted his upbringing. Fallon said he committed his life to God at a young age—"I saw real power." But then he got caught up in a web that led to his downfall. "I felt like I was a living, walking disease that gave birth to every seed of evil."

Angola is a place where Fallon believes he can get his life straightened out. He did not even object to toiling in the field at first: "I liked the fresh air, the exercise, the freedom to be out-of-doors, and the food was better." Yet it was only after recommitting his life to Christ that he began to accept what the prison offered. "Before then, I could have wound up in Camp J (in a solitary lockdown cell) or maybe even dead."

Accepted into the seminary, he now studies full-time. He said he is open to whatever God has in store for him when he graduates. "I'm preparing for the ministry that God has for my life."

He hopes God will lead him out of Angola. "We all have hope within us that we'll someday get out of here. We hope that God will free us to walk in our dreams." Yet he also knows he must be "real with God," to recognize that he may never leave the prison. "I'm praying that my desire to serve God would exceed my desire to get out of prison."

He admits that sometimes depression comes, "but only when I take my eyes off God. It's hard to be apart from my family. Sometimes I get the incarceration blues, particularly when I begin to have the desire for a wife and children, for a ministry outside of Angola."

Unlike other inmates who have spent many years in prison, Fallon, in his late twenties, has most of his life ahead of him. Some, observing his progress and impressed by his attitude and desire to serve God, wonder whether his zeal eventually will cool or even evaporate when it becomes apparent that he is not likely to ever leave Angola.

CHAPTER 14

"THEY KICKED ME OUT OF PRISON"

Then there are the few, the very few, who do leave.

As a teenager, Ashanti Witherspoon became a gang leader in Chicago. In 1971, he left the Windy City "on the run," believing the police were trying to arrest him for a crime he had not committed. Even after someone else confessed, Witherspoon rejected his attorney's recommendation to return and clear his name. Instead the brash young man settled in Louisiana. He soon was in far deeper trouble than he would have faced had he gone back to Chicago.

"In January 1972, I got involved in an armed robbery that turned into a shoot-out with the police," he explained. "I wounded two of them, but they survived. I got shot twice. One bullet passed through both of my upper legs. The other hit me in the head. It's still there, just inside my left temple."

A jury pronounced Witherspoon guilty, and the judge sentenced him to seventy-five years at Angola. The enormity of his sentence did not fully occur to the twenty-two-year old. "Like a lot of young people, I felt a sense of invincibility, that I wasn't going to be locked up that long, that I was going to get out. It was only after I had been at Angola for several years that I realized I might not ever be free again. At the very least, even with credit for good time, I was going to serve half of my term—thirty-seven and a half years. I'd be in my sixties by then."

He arrived at the prison in the spring of 1974. His reputation—as a guy who had wounded two cops in a shoot-out—seemed to protect him from the very outset. The prison had a horrible reputation. A federal judge had assumed jurisdiction over Angola, but the changes he ordered would take time.

"I remember coming down the road to Angola in a jail van with a certain sense of fear and apprehension. I had heard stories about the prison, how brutal it was—murders, rapes, even setting people on fire. But I also had that certain boldness, and I was determined to face the challenges that lie ahead. I was in an attack mode ready to defeat anyone who came at me."

Witherspoon spent forty-five days in the admitting unit, as the prison staff evaluated him and decided where he would live. At the beginning of his stint in the AU, a place where new cons had to prove themselves, a security officer and an inmate guard gave the new inmates an orientation. "There are not enough of us to protect you guys here," the security officer warned the new guys. His advice: "Find someone to make you a knife. If someone tries to hurt or take advantage of you, use it to kill him as quickly as possible. Chances are no one will ever inform on you, and you'll establish respect so no one will mess with you again."

Before the day was over, Witherspoon had two knives. "I didn't have problems in the AU. If you came to Angola for a violent crime, you already had earned a certain amount of respect. I had been in a shoot-out with the police—a real gun battle—and it was good to be from Chicago. That kept me mellow."

There were gangs in the admitting unit, young men from cities like New Orleans, Shreveport, and Baton Rouge. The out-of-state inmates "flocked" to Witherspoon. "We developed our own group to watch each other's back. That allowed us to sleep more soundly at night rather than having to sleep with one eye opened, the other eye closed."

After forty-five days in AU, Ashanti Witherspoon was transferred to Walnut 4, a dormitory in the main prison camp.

Like others before him, he faced taunts and harassment from veteran inmates. "They called me 'fresh fish.'" Fresh fish in a prison are new guys ripe for sexual bullying. And back then, unlike now, no fences protected the "fish" from the predators.

Witherspoon maneuvered the gauntlet carrying a box of personal items, prison-issued clothing and bedding for a cot. He ignored the jeers, although he admitted, "If I hadn't been psyched up, I might have taken off running to avoid getting attacked."

He soon made two friends—Otis Swift and Johnny Cool—and they protected him, handing him a knife and explaining how to keep it from being discovered when tactical officers carried out unannounced "shake-downs" to find contraband. He and the other two inmates became known as men who would be out on the walkway every Thursday when other new inmates arrived to "see that these guys had a knife. We became known as militants. We were against the prison administration. We practiced martial arts. We kept ourselves from becoming the targets of rapes or enticed into homosexuality."

When a shakedown team caught him with two knives, Witherspoon was locked up in a two-man cell, with only an hour outside—"tier time"—each day. "There was cell block warfare then. The guards would pay an inmate to take care of anyone they didn't like. They'd allow the guy to run into your cell and stab you or set you on fire. The men kept buckets of water under their beds so if someone had gasoline or lighter fluid, they could put out the fire if they got burned."

He continued to conceal a knife in his cell—made from scraps of tin that came from the license plate factory where prisoners produced license plates. "You could grind down the edges of the tin to make a sharp weapon."

On the cell block, Witherspoon became a jailhouse lawyer, filing lawsuits and pressing litigation to challenge what he and others considered "inhumane conditions." He did not accept responsibility for the crimes that sent him to Angola. "I blamed everybody for my predicament—white people, black people, judges, juries, my father, my mother, my domineering aunt, the police. Everybody but me."

But a subtle change was stirring in his soul. Inmate ministers would visit the cell block and talk to those in lockdown about their faith. "I was never disrespectful to anyone who was a minister. I would read the tracts they gave me and talk with them. God was working little by little, planting little nuggets in my life. I had heard about Jesus as a child, and I knew that verse, 'Train up a child in the way he should go, and when he is old he will never depart from it.'"

Still Witherspoon continued to blame everyone else for his imprisonment. He ignored a warning from an inmate in the cell next to his, "You've got seventy-five years . . . like serving a life sentence . . . we might all die here . . . we might as well change the way we act."

For Ashanti, it happened suddenly one night. "God really hit me. The reality was crystal clear. I knew that I might never get to see my daughter again (born while he was in Chicago). I might never get out. I might never fulfill my potential. I said to myself, 'How did you get into a place like this?' And I knew that only I was responsible for being in prison. I started crying, tears streaming down my face. Despite being in a prison where everything seemed so lost, where everything was so dark, I felt good, refreshed, alive at that moment. I knew God would always be there for me, and I prayed for Jesus to shape and mold me."

Yet he also knew that in such a dark place, it would take some doing to convince others of his change of heart.

Witherspoon determined that he would get out of his six-by-eight-foot cell in lockdown, but the security officers just looked at him and laughed. His efforts to return to a dormitory got nowhere. Then someone suggested a hunger strike. Ashanti, no fool, thought to himself, "They're just going to let you die if you don't eat." But his frustration led Ashanti to stop eating for twenty-seven days. It became a test of wills between him and the prison administration. They wanted to see how long the recalcitrant inmate would hold out.

Finally someone looked at the young man and saw something, something good and hopeful. A security officer with the title of "major" told him, "If you come off the hunger strike, I'll take a chance on you."

"He saw I wanted to change," says Ashanti. "I wondered if he really meant it. Another inmate assured me that the major was a man of his word, that I could be sure of him."

Witherspoon emerged from lockdown after fourteen months. But his struggle to find a future at Angola continued as security officers in the dormitory tormented him unmercifully. "They tried to push me to the point that I would explode. They knew I had a temper and knew martial arts. They would shake me down, force me to remove my clothing, and tear up my bedding looking for contraband. I kept saying, 'I've changed. I've made a commitment to Jesus, believe me.' Yet something inside of me still wanted to get back at the guards every day."

He wound up in an eight-week class designed to help an inmate "turn off the emotional button in your back, to keep you from making bad decisions and stop something before it happened." The teacher told Ashanti: "You're like a snake coiled to explode. You've got to try something else to cope with your frustration." Suddenly an answer came to Witherspoon, a way he could knock the guards harassing him off stride. "At first it didn't make any sense to me. I said, 'This can't work.' But I wound up praying about it that night at 3 a.m., and jumped up, shouting, 'This is going to work!'"

Instead of resisting, Witherspoon began welcoming the unannounced shakedowns in the mornings. "When they came into the dormitory, I'd already be naked and have my stuff ready for the search. I'd say, 'Come on in' and welcome them. I'd say, 'How was your weekend?' like I was talking to friends. I shook myself down, and they started mumbling to themselves.

"I felt good at that point. I even began calling the guards 'sir.' Before, I'd never call anyone 'sir.'" Soon some of the security officers, sensing his genuine change of attitude, admitted they had been trying to get Witherspoon to snap so he would get into trouble. "Then they started easing up on me."

In the years that followed, Ashanti became a positive inmate leader at Angola. But he made one more serious mistake, in the early 1980s. Believing he could enhance his standing as a "wheeler-dealer" in the prison, Witherspoon helped to fashion a homemade shotgun. He did not intend to use it, he said, but rather to turn it over to the security officers, whom, he believed, would credit him for uncovering a dangerous weapon.

"They found my fingerprint on the shotgun. I thought I had wiped it down well, but when they removed some tape that had been wound around the stock, they lifted a print fragment from one of my fingers." He got sent to Camp J, the harshest single-cell area at Angola, where he spent almost fifteen months before making his way back to a dormitory.

"I had become a prison politician, and I learned how power corrupts. I thought the shotgun incident would help me, but it backfired. It became apparent to me that God had put me in check. As I sat in a cell in Camp J, I told God I was sorry. I admitted that I had stopped working for Him, living for Him, that I had put Him aside to pursue my own agenda. I begged Him, 'I'm just asking for Jesus to be back in my life again—allow me to be in a position to glorify You.'"

In 1993 Ashanti Witherspoon began a succession of applications for parole. He first appeared before the parole board in 1994.

"They said, 'You shot two police officers' and denied my request." He filed six petitions and got turned down each time. Then he started filing lawsuits to win a resentencing, but none were granted. Finally, he sought a pardon from the governor, four times. Although the pardon board recommended him, the governor would not approve his release.

"At last I said to God, 'If You want me out, You'll have to be the One to let me out. If this is my ministry for the rest of my life, I promise I'll stay here and work for You.' Then I stopped working hard to get out."

In what might be considered a series of miracles, Witherspoon—now content to stay at Angola if that was what God had in mind for him—achieved the kind of "fame" that elevated his plight so that a handful of influential people became convinced he deserved to be paroled. A key event was the decision of Gabriel Films of Los Angeles, California, to film *The Farm,* a documentary about Angola. In one segment, Witherspoon described helping ordinary citizens learn CPR to save lives. By now a Class A trustee, Ashanti had become a member of a team that Angola allowed to travel outside to train in lifesaving techniques. The film achieved great popularity in the United States and was nominated for an Academy Award.

When the documentary was aired on the A&E channel, Witherspoon began receiving thousands of letters of support. "Everyone wanted to know why I was still incarcerated." Once again, he applied for a parole and was denied. That angered the film's producers, who began lobbying for his release. Burl Cain became one of Witherspoon's influential supporters, urging the parole board to reconsider Ashanti's petition. Then the husband of a woman who had done volunteer work at Angola and knew *The Farm* "didn't do justice" to Witherspoon joined her on a visit to the prison. The husband, a retired U.S. district attorney who had spent his life helping to send criminals into prison, and the inmate serving seventy-five years hit it off. "He met me without letting me know who he was. He told me, 'All my life I've sent people to jail. You're the first person I've met that I want to help get out.'"

When Witherspoon appeared once again before the parole board, its chairman, a former police chief who had investigated Ashanti's crime, asked Warden Cain and the former federal prosecutor to speak on his behalf. "The warden told the board how proud he was of me as a friend and how he'd gladly be my neighbor. He said he'd stake his career I would never get involved in crime again."

It takes a unanimous vote from the three board members for an inmate to be paroled. On June 18, 1999, after twenty-seven and a half years at Angola, Ashanti Witherspoon got all the votes.

"I was basically kicked out of prison."

Today he works on the staff of a church in Baton Rouge, serves on the Innocence Project in New Orleans, speaks frequently about prison life to groups around the country, and is involved in media projects. He is helping to develop a TV documentary featuring five persons who were innocent yet spent years in prison. Witherspoon points out that while there are support systems to help paroled or pardoned inmates, none exist for those wrongly convicted. He hopes the film will spur Louisiana legislators to pass a bill making it possible for these men and women to receive help and adequate compensation for the years of freedom they have lost.

Now in his mid-fifties, Ashanti is married, has a daughter, stepchildren, and eleven grandchildren. His daughter was three years old when he went to prison. What about the long years he missed?

"A part of me wishes it wouldn't have happened. My daughter went through bouts with law enforcement, although she's turned her life around. I was apart from all of my brothers. There was a long void in my life . . . a suffering that took place."

Yet he says, "My experience at Angola possibly saved me from some worse things."

CHAPTER 15

"HE KEPT HIS WORD"

When Burl Cain came to the Louisiana State Penitentiary in early 1995, inmates, aware of his reputation, worried that he would upset their lives. Cain had earned a reputation from his days at the Dixon Correctional Institution. "It was his way or no way," Ashanti Witherspoon recalled. The men at Angola wondered if the new warden would control areas of the prison that they continued to influence even as the prison underwent dramatic, positive changes.

"They thought, 'He's going to take everything from us,'" Witherspoon said.

Soon after he arrived, the former inmate added, Cain began to "cause serious ripples in the prison population. We began to hear rumbles of unrest. Of course, keep in mind that there is always going to be some period of unrest when a new warden comes. Warden Cain was just trying to reshape things he believed weren't right."

Worried that the warden's actions might trigger chaos, inmate leaders asked to meet with Cain "man-to-man." He agreed.

"We shot straight with him," Witherspoon said. "We told him, 'You're messing up here and here and here.' The warden said, 'Why didn't somebody tell me about this?' We helped him to understand the mentality of lifers, that there was a whole different mentality among them—this was their community."

The warden, Witherspoon said, called another session of all inmate leaders, the organization leaders, the religious leaders, and security staffers above certain ranks. "It was a jam-packed meeting. Warden Cain said, 'While I'm committed to making changes, I'm going to undo some things that I've done. I want to work together with you. God has me here for a purpose. I want to know what your thoughts are. I will try to help you.

"'I'm going to do what I can to make Angola better. I'm going to bring people here to see that you don't have horns and forked tails, welcome publicity, and show that there are men who are changing and someday might be able to return to society. I can't change the laws but I can bring programs to the prison that will make it better.'"

Then, according to Witherspoon, Burl Cain concluded, "God is going to live in this place."

The warden's speech resonated with some inmates but others were skeptical. They wondered if his actions would be consistent with his words. "I was watching his eyes, his body language," Witherspoon said. "I saw he was serious. Some of us who believed the warden meant what he said urged everyone to give him a chance."

The former inmate credits Cain with establishing what has become an expansive, continuing dialogue with the prisoners, which enables him to know what's on their minds. One tactic was to use the prison's radio station to communicate the message that inmates could voice their concerns without retribution. Cain allowed inmates to raise concerns, to ask, "Do you really have our backs?"

Witherspoon recalls that the warden's key administrators were expected to sit in on the radio sessions. Whenever he heard a good suggestion or change on air, Cain would send one of his assistant wardens to the office to type it up. "He'd institute new policies right then."

The former inmate also stressed that "almost overnight, God began using Warden Cain to open the doors to change. I heard him say again and again, 'The only lasting change in a man's heart is if he has God. Otherwise, whatever programs we offer the inmates are only going to make them into more intelligent criminals.'

"Under Burl Cain, Angola has become a fully developed, faith-based prison. He kept his word."

Other men still at Angola echo Ashanti Witherspoon's assessment of Warden Cain's impact:

"The warden tells us to be ourselves, to do what we're supposed to do, to be humble and not stumble. He treats us fairly. He's right when he says a man can't make a real change in his behavior unless he makes it with his heart."

"What has Burl Cain given us? Where do I begin? He's given us access to better equipment in the hobby shops. There are lots of clubs and organizations for the men to join. The rodeo has expanded. There are open call-outs for church services (permitting more inmates to participate). There is the seminary and other college opportunities. Lots of outside groups come in—the warden has opened the gates to them so they can see we're not awful people that they must fear. He gives us the opportunity to hold prison jobs that strengthen our belief in ourselves."

"He's been very supportive in all kinds of ways. He'll always talk with you, listen to you, give you feedback on your concerns."

"He tells us we are our brothers' keepers. That means we're supposed to watch out for each other, to consider Angola as our home, our neighborhood, our community."

"I thank God for Warden Cain. He's just a good person. He has a true love for people—just what Jesus had. He has adjusted the entire penitentiary to God. He's a vessel that God is using to reconcile the entire prison to Him. Society can learn a lot from Angola."

There are, of course, some inmates who have no opinion of Burl Cain or still do not believe he has their best interests at heart. His approach and programs do not reach them; for that matter, they probably would be dissatisfied or disgruntled no matter whatever efforts any warden put forth.

Cain has generated substantial interest from prison officials and legislators in other states, particularly in the South, where reaction to perceived breaching of the wall separating church and state is less vociferous than elsewhere. Many weeks Cain and others on his staff travel outside Louisiana to meet with those desiring to emulate Angola's transformation. A handful of legislators from Illinois, for example, spent several days with Cain and his staff at Angola to determine how they might convince their state prison administrators to experiment with aspects of the program. "They can do it," Cain declared not long ago, speaking of other states. "If it can happen here, it can happen anywhere."

But can the Angola experience—and success—be replicated elsewhere, without the energetic, white-haired warden with the accent as Louisiana as Tabasco and a growing public profile? "Other wardens say they're not outgoing like me and can't sell programs as I have," he says. "But they don't have to become clones of Burl Cain to make progress. They just have to be willing to keep trying and persevering even when they're confronted with crises that could easily derail what they are working hard to accomplish." It is also imperative that they have the support of their commissioners, Secretary of Corrections, and their legislature.

The modern history of America's prison experience reads like a chronicle of up-and-down efforts at reform. Often the efforts attract the attention of the media, always interested in an unusual story, or the opportunity to feature a positive inmate program that seems to be working. The media flock to the good-news story, and the inmates participating express their desire to make something of themselves.

An East Coast state initiated one such program a decade or so ago. Inmates serving long terms, but with records of good behavior, could be released from prison during weekdays to apprentice in local businesses so they might learn a trade that would help them succeed on the outside when they eventually were released. The program worked well and received considerable attention. Inmates fortunate enough to be selected to participate said the program made them feel like worthwhile human beings.

Then an inmate in the program went on a rampage at his training location and killed or hurt several workers who had been assisting him. Overnight, the program was suspended. The men who were benefiting found their hopes cruelly dashed, their opportunity vanished instantly because the resolve of the state's political leaders crumbled under the adverse publicity.

The politics of penology are simultaneously powerful and fragile. Supportive correctional officials, sometimes against their better judgment, may give enthusiastic wardens considerable latitude to experiment with programs and projects designed to make prisons safer and improve the lives of inmates. As long as everything goes smoothly, all connected in any way with the success are more than eager to bask in the glow of favorable publicity. But when something blows up, everyone runs for cover, and the men and women who envisioned, created, and devoted their energies to making it work are the only ones left to pick up the pieces.

Someone, usually the warden, takes the blame. The state's politicians keep on being politicians. And the new warden vows never to make the same mistakes as his luckless predecessor.

Burl Cain has become adept at negotiating the land mines of penal politics. Under his watch, the culture at Angola continues to grow in positive directions. He has escaped the fallout that accompanies the periodic crises that erupt from any maximum-security prison. He has grown stronger, more influential, and even more gifted at fostering a peaceful climate in the prison. Yet he takes little credit.

"I look up and ask God for wisdom. Without His wisdom, I'm not going to accomplish anything. Whatever happens, I know God is in control and He will give me what I need to meet any challenge."

But, of course, the spotlight often does fall on him. The engaging

Cain connects easily to people. A born storyteller, he has the knack for enthralling audiences with his tales of prison life. People in Louisiana recognize him and sometimes come up to him in restaurants and elsewhere to offer their thanks for the job he is doing.

What of the future? The warden hopes to remain at Angola for another decade. He and his energetic staff believe they still have much to accomplish and can assist the administrators of other prisons to transform as well. Yet they know that when all of them are gone, some programs could change, the inmates could face more restrictions and have fewer opportunities, the prison's environment could revert to an atmosphere resembling a human warehouse in which inmates are expected to obey— or else.

Burl Cain recognizes the possibility that a successor might attempt to undo much of what he has accomplished at Angola. That eventuality does not plague him because he believes his emphasis on true moral rehabilitation is creating a permanent change in inmate attitudes that no shift in programming can destroy.

"My legacy isn't bricks and mortar. It's what's in the hearts of men at Angola."

Burl Cain believes that as many as two thousand men at Angola have become committed followers of Jesus. He is thrilled God has used him to help accomplish that kind of moral rehabilitation. He believes whatever happens after he is no longer warden, his legacy will remain.

It is a legacy of men whose souls, though behind bars, are free.

ACKNOWLEDGMENTS

The author thanks Greg Thornton and William Thrasher, the leaders of Moody Publishers, for helping him to catch the vision of a transformed Angola Prison; Moody Publishers senior editor Betsey Newenhuyse; freelance editor Rebecca Jankowski; researcher and interviewer Anita Diann Cain Brown; Assistant Warden Cathy Fontenot; and Gary Young of the Angola Prison staff.

Cover Photo

Mark Saltz
Vance Jacobs

Photo Credits

Louisiana State Penitentiary:	1, 2, 24, 29, 32
Jim Whitmer:	3, 4, 5, 7, 9, 11, 13, 14, 15, 17, 18, 33, 36, 37, 38
Mark Saltz:	6, 8, 10, 12, 16, 19, 20, 21, 22, 23, 25, 26, 27, 28, 30, 31, 34, 35

Cover and Interior Design

Smartt Guys

ABOUT THE AUTHOR

Dennis Shere recently embarked on his third "career" serving as an attorney representing indigent defendants. Previously, he was a longtime newsman and senior officer with the Moody Bible Institute of Chicago.

A native of Cleveland, Shere graduated from Ohio University with bachelor and master's degrees in journalism. After a stint as a lieutenant in the U.S. Army in the 1960s, he became a reporter in Dayton, Ohio. After teaching journalism for a year at a state university in Ohio, he became financial editor and later city editor of a newspaper in Detroit. He returned to Dayton as editor of the morning newspaper and was promoted to publisher of a sister newspaper in Springfield, Ohio. He describes the difference between serving as an editor and a publisher this way: "The editor stands on a soapbox; the publisher steadies it." After serving as publisher of the newspaper in Dayton, he joined the Moody Bible Institute as managing editor of *Moody Monthly,* its magazine. He then became general manager of the Institute's media operations, including what is now Moody Publishers and Moody Broadcasting.

In 2000, Shere chose to pursue a longtime dream of attending law school. After retiring from Moody, he graduated from the DePaul University College of Law in Chicago and passed the Illinois bar in the summer of 2003. He worked a year for the Death Penalty Trial Assistance Division of the Illinois State Appellate Defender's Office. He currently is an assistant public defender in Kane County, Illinois.

Cain's Redemption is Shere's first book. A budding novelist, he also has written drafts of two stories based on his past as a newsman and his present as an attorney.

Of the "careers" he has had, he remarks: "God has been gracious to allow me to enjoy a lifetime of challenging and exciting professional pursuits."

We hope you enjoyed this product from
Northfield Publishing. Our goal at Northfield
is to provide high quality, thought provoking
and practical books and products that connect
truth to the real needs and challenges of
people like you living in our rapidly changing
world. For more information on other books
and products written and produced from a
biblical perspective write to:

Northfield Publishing
215 West Locust Street
Chicago, IL 60610